**FOR PEOPLE WITH THAT SPECIAL
PIONEERING SPIRIT**
people who take pride in creating something that's
truly their own, people who want to get the most
for their money without sacrificing space, style, or
convenience—here is

THE LOG HOUSE BOOK

Can just anyone build a three- or four-bedroom
house with a few tools and a little help from some
friends? Yes! And whether you're the real
back-to-nature type, ready to go out and clear the
land, chop down and prepare your own logs, and
construct a house that is uniquely you; or whether
you're the kind of person who might find a log
house kit the perfect solution to limited time and
carpentry experience, this do-it-yourselfer's guide
to the home of your dreams offers you step-by-step
instructions and advice that will make the building
of your own house an exciting and fulfilling
experience.

JACK KRAMER is the author of over 100 books devoted
to gardening, crafts, and remodeling. His books include
the bestselling *1,000 Beautiful Houseplants* and *Your
Homemade Greenhouse*. Mr. Kramer resides in Marin
County, California.

THE LOG HOUSE BOOK

BY
JACK KRAMER

Drawings by Berne Holman

A PLUME BOOK
NEW AMERICAN LIBRARY
TIMES MIRROR
NEW YORK, LONDON AND SCARBOROUGH, ONTARIO

NAL BOOKS ARE AVAILABLE AT QUANTITY DISCOUNTS WHEN USED TO
PROMOTE PRODUCTS OR SERVICES. FOR INFORMATION PLEASE WRITE TO
PREMIUM MARKETING DIVISION, THE NEW AMERICAN LIBRARY, INC.,
1633 BROADWAY, NEW YORK, NEW YORK 10019.

All drawings are by Berne Holman.

Library of Congress Catalog Card Number: 78-71260

 PLUME TRADEMARK REG. U.S. PAT. OFF. AND FOREIGN COUNTRIES
REGISTERED TRADEMARK—MARCA REGISTRADA
HECHO EN WESTFORD, MASS., U.S.A.

SIGNET, SIGNET CLASSICS, MENTOR, PLUME, MERIDIAN and
NAL BOOKS are published in the United States by
The New American Library, Inc.,
1633 Broadway, New York, New York 10019,
in Canada by the New American Library of Canada Limited,
81 Mack Avenue, Scarborough, Ontario M1L 1M8,
in the United Kingdom by The New English Library Limited.
Barnard's Inn, Holborn, London, ECIN 2 JR, England

First Plume Printing, March, 1979

5 6 7 8 9 10 11 12

PRINTED IN THE UNITED STATES OF AMERICA

To B. L. H.

ACKNOWLEDGMENTS

We wish to thank the following manufacturers for their cooperation in the preparation of this book:

Alpine Log Homes, Victor, Mont.

Alta Industries, Ltd., Halcottsville, N.Y.

Boyne Falls Log Homes, Boyne Falls, Mich.

Building Logs Inc., Gunnison, Colo.

National Log Company, Thompson Falls, Mont.

Northeastern Log Homes, Inc., Groton, Vt.

Real Log Homes Inc., Missoula, Mont.

Vermont Log Buildings, Inc., Hartland, Vt.

Wilderness Log Homes, Plymouth, Wisc.

CONTENTS

THE
LOG
HOUSE
BOOK

INTRODUCTION: NOT ONLY FOR HOMESTEADERS

The log cabin appeared early in America's history and has proved to be a worthy structure. The basic plan is simple, the construction is generally easy, the cost is minimal, and the end product is durable. There is nothing fancy or sophisticated about the log house. It is, however, a natural solution to the problem of housing and to the soaring costs of traditional building, so it is not surprising that we are experiencing a renaissance in the log type structure.

You can build your own log house—and in this book we show you several styles you can tackle yourself—or you can purchase a kit-type log cabin with all the pieces and assemble them as you do a commercial greenhouse. You can cut your own logs—not so far-fetched—or buy precut logs. There are many woods to use, many styles to choose. And you can erect a dwelling—a very suitable and durable one—for as little as $10,000, or much less if you make everything yourself.

Basic floor plans and styles of log houses differ depending upon the site and the use, and we cover many different situations here. What you choose depends on your own specific situation, but whatever it is, the log house offers economy and reliability. Once built it is built to stay. More important, perhaps, the log house greatly˙ reduces costs of heating and cooling artificially; it has a great many advantages and is basically a house that is in harmony with nature, not against it. As such, it offers a happy solution to the problem of housing for those who want individual and distinctive housing at low cost.

It is definitely a self-sufficient structure you can make yourself and enjoy doing it.

1

THE LOG CABIN

When we think of a house of logs we think of a log cabin somewhere in the woods where pioneers lived. That is the way the history books present it, but we have come a long way since then. For decades log houses were out of favor except with those select few who chose to live with nature. Today, the log house is making a strong comeback because it is economical, easy to build, and functional. It is a natural answer to building a home. The log house is very much with us as a structure for living now.

Why Build One?

The revolution of the flower children of the 1960s created a new way of life for many people who took to the woods, who learned and are learning to be self-sufficient. From the craftsperson's homemade house, log or otherwise, we found we could build our own dwellings, many times better than professionals. After all, a house is a personal place—your own place. Your own log house is unique and possesses a magic that no builder's house can have. It also encourages a way of life that is becoming desirable to more and more people.

1. *This homemade log house is small but adequate and was built for under $10,000. It was hand done from foundation to roof.* (PHOTOGRAPH BY MATTHEW BARR)

There is also the big plus of cost. The log house is far less expensive to build than the conventional dwelling, which is generally beyond the average person's income. It is the one way to have a custom-built house if you are on a limited budget.

The log house requires less framing and construction than the frame house. Solid log walls provide more insulation against cold and heat than frame walls, and in moderate climates you may be able to do without additional insulation and still enjoy both comfort and low heating costs. And maintenance can be very much less expensive and time-consuming than it often is for conventional houses. (For additional information on insulation see Chapter 10.)

Location

The ideal spot for a log house is in a wooded area or in the mountains—any place where there is privacy and elbow room. However, more and more log houses (usually kit-type homes) are appearing in more settled areas on small lots.

2. A prefabricated kit house in a simple cabin style and ideally situated on the forest edge. (COURTESY ALTA INDUSTRIES)

3. Of heavy logs and very well done, this handsome log house in a suburban area was done by hand by the owner and a friend.
(PHOTOGRAPH BY MATTHEW BARR)

The log "cabin" is no longer restricted to the mountains or forest.

In its new role in today's architecture, the log house has greatly expanded from its original cabin plan to become an all-year residence. It is no longer just an occasional retreat. You can build a log home in almost any climate from California to New England, and it will be a functional and durable home for your family. The log house is not for everyone; there are many people who prefer different types of architecture. This is fine, but for the thousands of you who admire the log home for its beauty and functional efficiency, try one.

Can You Do It Yourself?

The idea of building your own home may panic you, but as we said, the log house is easier to construct than the conventional house. Some carpentry is necessary, but you certainly do not have to be a professional. If you are reasonably handy with tools and like working with wood, you can make your own dwelling. The actual construction takes time and some know-how but is not that difficult; lifting and hauling the logs are, however, problems, but not insurmountable.

I have friends who are not carpenters by any means—one is a draftsman, the other a musician—but each has, in a short time, constructed his own log home with the help of a few friends to move and lift timbers.

Traditionally, the log house was built from timbers on the land. People cut the trees and prepared the logs. Today, you can buy the logs—it is more costly, but saves a great deal of time.

Sawmills sell logs, and some lumberyards in outlying areas also carry them. Any lumberyard should be able to order them for you; explain what you are doing and the yard will help you find the logs you need. You can even arrange to buy logs from someone else's land or, as was the case with an architect I know, buy surplus logs from the telephone company. You can also read the classified ads in small-town papers for sales of logs.

Cost

If you start from scratch and build your own log house, you can probably get a 1,000-square-foot house for about

4. *This kit house of about 800 square feet has concrete foundation wall; the small house is well placed on site.*
(PHOTOGRAPH BY BERNE HOLMAN)

$10,000. The house may not be a palace, and it may be small, but it will be a charming personal place in which you will want to live. The crafted touch will be evident, and the satisfaction of saying "I did it myself" is tremendous for the ego, as are the savings in dollars.

If you buy a kit house—a prefabricated house with all the log parts (and these are fine)—you save all the labor of cutting and hewing. And with the dozens of models available you can probably find a design that suits your taste. This house will still have the crafted touch, still be charming, and of course will be properly engineered. A 1,000-square-foot kit house at this writing costs about $10,000. However, to this you must add the cost of foundation, wiring, plumbing, dimensional lumber (for floors), and so on. This complete house will probably end up costing about $20,000. (See Chapter 9.)

Either way—doing it all yourself or buying a kit house and putting it together—you save buckets of money because a conventional framed 1,000-square-foot house today costs about $50,000, plus and plus.

5. This hand-hewn, cabin-type log house is surrounded by towering tress—a fine vacation house. (PHOTOGRAPH BY MATTHEW BARR)

6. *Nestled in the hills, this stockade-type log house, built in the late 1800s, still stands.* (PHOTOGRAPH BY BERNE HOLMAN)

2

THE SITE

Your log house's floor plan and its exterior appearance can be whatever you want them to be, depending upon your tastes and how you want the house to function in your life. But you may find yourself restricted as to choice of site, and once you have a site, you will have to study it carefully to determine the best placement of the house on it. For example, if you want the house to benefit from cool summer breezes yet be protected from winter storms, you may find only one spot on your land that is right.

You must consider wind, sun, and shade. You want a house that will get the winter sun but be shaded by trees from summer sun. You want your house positioned in such a way that it has a good northwestern windbreak of trees or shrubs. Because the log house is a natural house, it should be placed naturally to work with nature rather than against her.

Of course, no matter how you place the house on the site, you still will be governed by the lot size and its terrain—whether it is hilly or level. Accessibility and proximity to daily activities are other considerations, as is cost. All factors must be considered before you start any planning or the end results will be unpredictable.

No matter what kind of house you are building—log or conventional—the site is of the utmost importance. Thus it pays to search and search until you find the place that suits you perfectly. Alas, in most cases the dream site rarely materializes, so some compromises must be made. If the log house is to be that dream cabin in the mountains or that sylvan retreat in the woods, you should have some general knowledge of buying country property. You should know, if you buy raw land, whether you have to put a road in, excavate, and fill. And there must be provisions for water and electricity as well.

If the log house is not in a country setting—and today it need not be—you'll have fewer problems, of course. But even in the suburbs you must consider the type of land and its size, cost, and taxes, subsurface conditions, and the utilities available. Buying land for the conventional house is covered in many other books, so here we will deal only with woodland sites and agricultural land.

7. Occupying an ideal site on a hill, this large log house offers all the conveniences of the conventional home. It is a kit house offered by Alta Industries. (COURTESY ALTA INDUSTRIES)

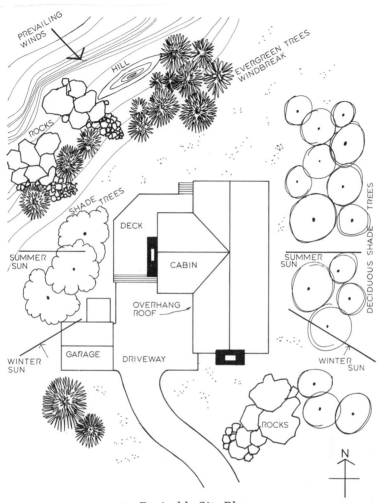

1. *Desirable Site Plan*

Agricultural Land

If you want to do some vegetable gardening and keep your own animals, you will have to seek land that is zoned for agricultural use. You can do the "farming" on 2 or 20 acres; it all depends upon what you can afford and how

[11]

8. In the forest, in a cleared area, a simple handmade log house has an ideal setting; it seems a part of the landscape and is situated so trees buffer northwest storms. (PHOTOGRAPH BY BERNE HOLMAN)

much you want to do. No matter what land you buy, remember that you will have to clear it. If there is a level cleared area for the house, all the better, but in your cost estimates consider the cost of clearing the land for your use and for the site. Depending upon the terrain, this can be inexpensive or costly. Naturally, level land is best to work with.

Remember road access and such. This is more important than you think. A house you can't get to is not much fun. There must be a suitable road, and if one does not exist you will be putting it in yourself or paying someone to do it.

Woodland

The cabin in the woods is a common dream, so wooded sites are always picked off first. These sites are beautiful and

9. *Forested settings make handsome canvas for log houses. This one is reached by a remote path and is in harmony with the landscape.* (PHOTOGRAPH BY BERNE HOLMAN)

have character, and log houses look stunning in such locations. (Also, if you are building from scratch, you will be looking for a good timber stand.) About 5 acres or more—ideally, 10 acres—is a handsome wooded site. If you buy a wooded site, be sure you can cut your trees, because many areas restrict tree cutting to the initial cutting for the home site.

With wooded land, be sure you know what you are in for, because cutting trees is not for everyone, and having them cut commercially can cost a great deal of money. So when buying wooded land, look for a site that has a naturally cleared area where the house might be. Then you can modify the site to your taste by removing a few trees and landscaping.

As with all property, check out grades and levels, accessibility to roads and water, and, of course, taxes and costs. Remember that taxes on unimproved land may be very low, but once you build your log house on it, they may rise considerably.

Permits, Licenses, and So Forth

As with all home building, except perhaps in the remotest areas, you will need a building permit and have to know the local building code, especially if you are building your own. Many areas require an architect's plans, even if you do your own construction. Some areas ask only for sketches. This varies from state to state. Before you buy your land, be sure to check with the building inspector or other appropriate authority to find out just what you can and cannot build and how you must adhere to existing building codes.

Climatic Considerations

Just what kind of log house you build greatly depends upon the climate. In severe winter climates you have to build a different type of house than you would in temperate areas. The log house is naturally a practical house for severe winter areas; because it is solid wood it holds heat relatively well, fits the landscape well, and with proper roof design it can accommodate heavy snow loads.

Checking out the climate of a given area is not difficult. The USDA supplies weather maps that give mean temperatures, rainfall, and snowfall; it is wise to check out this material. Write to U.S. Department of Agriculture, Washington, D.C., 20402. The climate gives you a good clue as to road use, accessibility to the main highway, and other important factors. If the temperature in your area can drop to 40 below zero, you can design your log house accordingly, with extra insulation and suitable paths, and can situate it to give it protection from winds and storms.

Make sun your ally, not your enemy, by positioning the house properly. A west-facing placement is good (if there is nothing blocking your view to the west) because that leaves a sizable wall area facing south. The low winter sun will help warm the house, so you will not have to burn as much fuel. To get the most from the sun, limit the windows on the east and west sides; place most windows on the south. To control the sun effectively, plant deciduous trees on both east and west sides. The trees will provide shade in the summer but allow the winter sun to penetrate.

If there are no windbreaks on the north and west exposures, plant three rows of shrubs to really buffer the house from storms. (These plantings can reduce your winter heating bills by one-third.) And do not forget to plan for roof overhangs; in the summer they effectively shade the house, and in the winter, when the sun is at a low angle, they let light in.

Winter wind can be a bitter enemy, but if you plant evergreen hedges you will bless your foresight. Other wind buffers, such as fences and screens, may also be erected for winter protection.

View

The view from your house should be pleasing and unobstructed. If trees are in the way, removing them or even just topping them will be expensive, so place the house where a minimum of such work will be necessary. However, when you are dealing with views, you are dealing with compromises. For example, suppose your best view would be to the north. Unfortunately, in noncoastal regions storms generally come in from the north and west (in coastal regions storms often come in from the sea). But you can compromise and still get some view by *not* putting the house smack dab in line with the winds.

Resist the temptation to put in large picture windows. These windows are inevitably drafty, and they really are not in character with the log house. Smaller windows are more charming and more in keeping with the overall design of log buildings.

Grading

Proper grading, the moving and shaping of the contour of the lot, is an important part of any home building to control erosion, ensure proper water drainage, and provide road accessibility to the property. You can change the grading by putting in fill. Grading and leveling should be done first and carefully considered. If your lot is already level, it will not need much grading; sloping or hilly lots need a fair amount of grading.

On a small site, grade with a rake and shovel; this is hard but not impossible work. Break up stones, remove trash, and then smooth and level mounds and hollows. On a larger lot, rent a bulldozer or front-end loader. If the existing land level is high, you must shear it off; if the level is low, you must fill in the land.

Leveling, which is done after the grading, is smoothing and leveling the ground so there are no hollows or hills. Hollows create bogs of run-off water, and rises are unsightly. The land must be graded to slope away from the house and carry water to the nearest watercourse. Be sure the slope is in one direction, either toward the front or toward the rear. If the water runoff is more than the ground can handle without causing erosion, dig ditches at the edge of the property. The ditches will collect and channel water into a lower area, where it can then seep away.

Surface water must be kept moving, but if it moves too fast it creates gullies, and if it moves slowly it creates bogs. Provide a gradual slope, with the earth slightly pitched away from the house. Allow 2 inches to every 10 feet.

Until you have had some rain or spring thaw, it will be difficult to determine just how much work has to be done to provide adequate drainage. In a new site that has been excavated and filled in, natural drainage patterns have been interrupted. You must guess at the natural slope of the land—where water would run off—and grade accordingly.

Miscellaneous, But Very Important

In the excitement of building your log house you may forget such incidentals as accessibility, utilities, and so on. Yet these are vital factors, so you better determine just where the power is coming from, where the septic tank should go, and how you're going to get to the house before your building is up.

First, if you are building in snow country, try to determine if the property is accessible year-round. Call local authorities and find out who maintains the public road closest to your site and whether it is maintained all winter.

Also remember that there must be a road or at least a driveway to your house. In some cases you will be building the road. Be sure the terrain is not too steep, and make sure it will be accessible during snowstorms. Consider spring runoff, which can flood a road, and be sure there is space at the house for cars to turn around in (backing down a road is no pleasure). Road building is expensive (about $10 a lineal foot), but you cannot do without one.

3

DESIGN

If you are building a log house, your tastes may be simple—a one-room structure—or elaborate—a six-room house. Generally, the log house you build yourself will be an average size of, say, four rooms, with a loft perhaps. More sophisticated houses of logs are more difficult for amateurs to construct from scratch, but with a kit house with all pieces furnished, size is much less of a problem.

Just how you use the log house is another consideration. Will it be an all-year home or a vacation retreat? The use will dictate the design. So, whether you want a small or a large house, planning of space is essential.

Just as essential as the floor plan is the outside design of the dwelling. Is it to be a one-story or a two-story home? Will it have a gable roof, an eaved roof, or what? The styles of log houses vary considerably, depending upon their use and their total environment.

Authenticity

The purist will disagree with the idea of combining the best of the old with the best of the new. This writer, however, believes that by using the basic principles of both the authentic log house and the more traditional types of

10. *A typical log house—neither large nor small—makes a hand-some home in a beautiful wooded setting. The rectangular gabled design is popular.* (COURTESY BUILDING LOGS, INC.)

building, as well as modern tools, the results are very satisfactory. Why not have the best of two worlds? Of course it is possible to construct the log cabin without power tools, without new types of insulation, without indoor plumbing, and so forth. This might be fine for some people, but for most people who want the beauty of the log-type house and the conveniences of today, it is better to borrow a little from both worlds.

For example, the flooring in a log house may be log joists (flattened), but dimensional framing can save a lot of time, although it does cost slightly more than authentic log flooring. It is also perhaps easier than log construction. Some people might even prefer an earth-packed floor, and this is fine for them. However, most people will want both to preserve the character of the log house and to use some of the modern ways to build it, and this, to me, is the best approach.

Styles

Working with logs allows you great flexibility in the design of your home. You are *not* limited to a standard rectangular house. The house can be L-shaped or even octagonal; it can be two stories or one; a split-level or a stockade type (logs running vertically). There is really little limitation other than cost and the space available for

11. *This homemade log house follows no particular design and the roof line is most unusual; still it works well and looks fine.* (PHOTOGRAPH BY MATTHEW BARR)

12. The L-shaped design is frequently seen; it is not as easy to build as a rectangular house but makes for a good floor plan. (PHOTOGRAPH BY MATTHEW BARR)

building. Most importantly, design with function in mind. Consider alternate floor plans (we show you three in our drawings) and position windows and doors where you want them for view or privacy, as the case may be.

The logs you use will of course determine the design and size of the house. Some logs are slender, others heavy; some long, some short. Remember that if you are working alone you will not be able to handle, say, a 50-foot log for a wall. Two people can, however, handle a dry 35-foot log.

As mentioned before, the size of your log house depends on many things. Will you be there all year? Part of the year? Weekends? In each case the use of the house will determine the size and number of the rooms. And do not scoff at the conventional one-room structure. A large cabin, say 30 × 35 feet, can actually, with intelligent planning, be four rooms: living room, kitchen, bedroom, and bath.

Before construction begins, determine the position of interior walls, the fireplace, and doors and windows.

Houses can be made with a combination of materials as well, for example, of logs and brick or logs and stone. These combinations look handsome and retain the appealing rustic appearance of the log house. There is a certain charm in any log house, whether small or large, made of all logs or of logs combined with other materials.

Look at conventional houses in magazines and visualize them built with logs. Eventually you will come up with your own house, the one you personally like and want. Do not be swayed by architects or designers, but do pay heed to their suggestions about construction details, structural loads, and, especially, plumbing and electrical data.

Make sketches and plans, and if you prefer, consult with an architect about day-to-day living space for your log house. Today, most architects are aware of the advantages and popularity of the log house and will help you make sketches. (Note: Always make fee arrangements beforehand. Basically, the log house is easier to design than the conventional one, so the architect's fee should be lower than what it would be for a "regular" house.)

The Retreat Cabin

For a modest price you can build a one- or two-room cabin with considerable rustic charm. The floor plan for this cabin can be a large living-dining area with a kitchen to the side and a bedroom with bath at the rear of the living room. A simpler solution is a lean-to kitchen and one large room with perhaps a sleeping loft; this is a popular plan and looks good. There is enough space to move around in, but not so much that the cabin is expensive to build. The 800-square-foot, two-bedroom, modernized log cabin has the bedrooms separated by a bath, and a large living-dining room with an adjacent kitchen.

If your log house is to be for occasional use, such as weekends, any one of these three plans works fine and involves minimal interior-wall construction.

The All-Year Log House

If your log house is going to be a permanent residence (and many people are doing this now), make it comfortable. Put in everything you normally would have in a conventional house. Make your bedrooms large, and pay attention to traffic flow. Be sure the kitchen is easily accessible to the dining or living room. And do put in enough space for sitting and eating in the kitchen; this will make the kitchen cozy and inviting.

The all-year log house will probably need about 1,400 square feet to make it a comfortable residence. Cost is higher, of course, and you will need more time to build the house. Again, the plan of the house should depend on the uses you have in mind for it.

2. *Floor Plans*

If the log house is to be a permanent residence or occupied most of the year, its style can be any of the traditional designs that apply to conventional houses: Colonial, split level, ranch, L-shaped, Cape Cod. Let's look at these various styles:

Ranch style: Everything is on one floor; relatively easy to build and expand.

Cape Cod: Classical design in which second floor begins at the roof line. Usually has dormers and is very charming.

Gambrel roof Cape Cod: The gambrel roof design has a steep pitch on the lower part, a shallower pitch to the peak. Very handsome, but roof details are complex.

Colonial: A general term for a two-story house; usually has a hip roof (roof pitch coming down on all sides). Makes for good space, but again roof is difficult to build.

Split level: The upper floor usually is half again as high as the lower floor. Somewhat difficult to build.

There are other styles and designs of houses; this is a sampling. Magazines on building and plans are at newsstands and you can look through these. If you are buying a kit house, you will find that the manufacturers offer catalogs with descriptions of different styles of log houses, one of which would surely suit your needs.

4

WOOD FOR YOUR HOUSE

Pine, spruce, and poplar are considered the best woods to build a log house with, but other woods can be used as long as you know their strength and workability. The bending strength of any wood is very important, because floor joists and rafters are loaded laterally. Bending strength varies from wood to wood. The hardwoods (oak, hickory, white ash, beech) are very resistant to breaking; however, the softwoods (white cedar, pine, redwood, cypress, hemlock, red cedar), called conifers or evergreens, which do not have as good bending strength as the hardwoods, are straighter, rounder, more uniform in size, resistant to shrinkage and decay, and very parasite-resistant, and thus they are preferred over the hardwoods. White oak, sugar maple, yellow birch, and hickory are excellent hardwoods, but they are somewhat prone to decay. However, this problem can be remedied by the use of the proper preservatives.

Thus, in order to select the best kind of wood for your needs, consider the workability, bending strength, and ability to resist decay and shrinkage. And always keep an eye on cost. Usually, if a place has an abundance of one wood, that wood will be cheaper than a wood in short supply—it usually pays to buy the surplus type of wood, to save money.

13. *The amateur craftsman may want to cut his own logs; here they are ready for use.* (PHOTOGRAPH BY BERNE HOLMAN)

Getting Logs

It's ideal to have your own stand of timber so you can cut and prepare your own logs. Unfortunately, this situation rarely exists, or, if it does, most likely you do not have the time to cut your own logs. If yours is the typical situation, it is likely you will be buying your logs. Although this is more costly than doing it yourself, having the logs prepared and delivered is worth the extra money. You will still be saving yourself plenty of money when you build the house yourself, anyway.

You can sometimes get logs from a local construction site,

but usually you will have to buy them direct from a sawmill or lumber company. Just what kinds of logs you buy makes a big difference in terms of money and usability, so read on.

Quick Reference List of Woods

Beech is very strong, has low shrinkage, but does not resist decay very well.

Black locust is a good all-round wood, with low shrinkage, high strength, and a high resistance to decay and moisture.

14. *Board lumber and logs awaiting the builder. The board lumber will be used for framing the sill walls.* (PHOTOGRAPH BY BERNE HOLMAN)

[29]

Black spruce is fairly easy to work with and has low shrinkage, but has low resistance to decay.

Cypress is fairly easy to work with, has low shrinkage, and has a high resistance to decay.

Douglas fir is a general all-round wood with medium shrinkage, low decay resistance, and good strength.

Hemlock is tough to work with, but has low shrinkage and does not resist decay too well.

Hickory is hard to work with, has very high shrinkage, and has low resistance to decay.

Maple is tough to work with, has high shrinkage, and has good bending strength. Its resistance to decay and moisture is so-so.

Pines of various types—white pine, jack pine, and red pine—are easy to work with, have little shrinkage, and have exceptional bending stress. However, they do not resist decay or moisture too well.

Poplar is easy to work with, has a medium degree of shrinkage, and has low resistance to decay.

Red cedar is a good all-round wood that is easy to work with, has very low shrinkage, and is very resistant to decay and termites.

Red oak and white oak are hard to work with and have high shrinkage, but resist decay fairly well. These are both very strong woods with excellent bending strength.

Spruce is fairly easy to work with, has low shrinkage, and is fairly decay-resistant, but is not a particularly strong wood.

White ash has high shrinkage and a low resistance to decay, but is a very strong wood.

White cedar is easy to work with, has low shrinkage, and is fairly decay-resistant; however, it does not have good bending strength.

Kinds of Logs

No matter which wood you buy, try to get logs that are straight and without too many branches; crooked or sharply tapered logs can drive you crazy when you start building. You will also need some short logs for rafters.

If you make a floor plan first and know the size of your house, you can determine how many feet of logs you will

15. *This closeup of a corner of a hand-hewn log house shows the effort of the builder. Small 4-inch-diameter logs are used for detailing and heavier logs for the walls.* (PHOTOGRAPH BY MATTHEW BARR)

16. *This photograph shows the typical log used in small homemade cabins. Note handsome chimney stack at left.* (PHOTOGRAPH BY MATTHEW BARR)

need. The *average* size of a log is based upon the diameters of its butt and top ends added and then divided by 2. For example, a log 14 inches at the butt and 8 inches at the top averages 11 inches: $14 + 8 = 22 \div 2 = 11$.

The best logs to work with are those that have been fully dried and seasoned, because such logs will not shrink or split later. Peel the logs, and then stack them so they do not touch each other. To season the logs, cover them with hay or straw to protect them from weather. If logs stand this way for about a year, they are ideal for building purposes.

Most logs you buy are *not* peeled, and those you cut obviously need peeling too. Peeling hastens drying, discourages parasites, and gives the logs a clean, smooth, attractive look. You should peel logs in the spring, preferably after they have been cut in the winter. The bark is looser and thus easier to get off then; if you try to peel logs cut in the spring, you will have a good deal of sap running all over the logs and yourself. To peel a log, lift one end of the log off the ground. Make wooden props for the logs so the logs do not roll off. Use a peeling spud and a drawknife (see Chapter 6).

Preservatives

After logs are peeled, they should be treated with preservatives to increase their resistance to decay and

17. *Small-diameter logs—4 or 5 inches—are used in this kit-type house; the effect is more tailored than with hand-hewn logs.* (COURTESY BUILDING LOGS INC.)

insects. There are numerous insects and fungi that attack logs, but if the logs are treated properly, you will never have any problems. A coat of old-fashioned tar creosote is a good preservative. It penetrates deeply and has a good dark color, but it does smell bad, and the smell persists for weeks or months.

Use water-borne preservatives for wood that will not be in direct contact with the ground. There are many such preservatives; they are all made from more or less the same ingredients. Ask your lumber dealer to recommend a brand.

Dipping the logs into a tank filled with preservative is fast and efficient. But finding a tank or trough long enough to accommodate the logs is the trick. You can piece together some 50-gallon oil barrels, or make a wooden trough from plywood. Soak the logs at least three minutes and then roll them in the preservative.

You can go mad if you spray or paint logs with preservatives; it takes an enormous amount of time and you never really get total coverage or deep penetration. Soak and treat all logs before working with them; after construction you can paint various ends and cuts. See Chapter 11 for more information on wood and preserving it.

Plywood

You will use some plywood sheets for window frames, flooring, walls, and so forth. Plywood is several layers of veneer (thin layers of wood) laid perpendicular to each other and bonded together with synthetic resin glue. The thickness of the plies varies, depending upon what the plywood will be used for. Plywood is stronger, because of the alteration of grain direction in the layers, than solid wood of the same thickness.

Marine and exterior plywood is available in various grades—that used for subfloor and siding is generally specified as C-D. It does have blemishes. The difference is the glue.

Cheap plywoods have core veneers of inferior quality, the joints between edges may not be perfectly mated, and the wood may have knots or patches in it. Always select plywood in person rather than ordering by phone. Use marine-grade or exterior-type plywood; these are bonded with moisture-resistant glue. Plywood comes with both surfaces sanded or unsanded; unsanded plywood is not generally satisfactory because it is difficult to work with. The standard size for plywood sheets is 4 × 8 feet, but they are available in larger sizes.

Dimensional Lumber

Some log houses are made entirely of logs; others use dimensional lumber for framing floors and so on. Dimensional or board lumber is standard lumber that comes in boards: 2 × 6 inches, 2 × 8 inches, and so forth. It is purchased at lumberyards, and just as logs may be cedar or pine, board lumber comes in various woods. Usually, Douglas fir is used for interior work because it is a good all-purpose wood with good strength.

Dimensional lumber comes in various grades. Clear heartwood, A grade, and common grade are surfaced on both sides to a smooth finish. Select heart or construction heart may come from the mill with a rough surface and is generally fine for most work. Even within the grades of lumber there are variations, so it is best to select wood personally. Also, sometimes wood is warped or out of square, and this can cause havoc for the amateur builder.

And remember that dimensional lumber is sold in *nominal* sizes; actual size is somewhat smaller. Thus a 2 × 6-inch board is actually 1½ × 5½ inches. When ordering, specify wood as to type (Douglas fir), size (2 × 6 inches), and length.

Dimensional lumber is easier to use for joists and flooring than logs so if time is more a problem than money it makes sense to use it. Some craftsmen may claim this is cheating and the authenticity of the log structure is diminished if you resort to dimensional lumber. Perhaps so, but it does do the job and saves a great deal of time.

5

LOGS, JOINTS, CAULKING

Working with logs is adventuresome and fun, because there is much craftsmanship and ingenuity involved. True, you will not be creating sculptured pieces, but working with your hands to make notches, splices, and various log shapes is downright intriguing. You can use logs just as they come from the supplier, but you are going to have to cut and carve the logs to make all the pieces fit together. Remember as a

18. Log joinery with a tight seal; a V-ended log was used with a round log to achieve snug fit. (PHOTOGRAPH BY MATTHEW BARR)

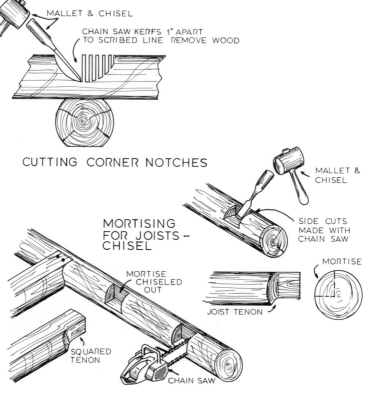

MALLET & CHISEL

CHAIN SAW KERFS 1" APART
TO SCRIBED LINE REMOVE WOOD

CUTTING CORNER NOTCHES

MALLET &
CHISEL

MORTISING
FOR JOISTS –
CHISEL

SIDE CUTS
MADE WITH
CHAIN SAW

MORTISE
CHISELED
OUT

MORTISE

JOIST TENON

SQUARED
TENON

CHAIN SAW

MORTISING FOR JOISTS – CHAIN SAW

3. Mortising

child how you fitted together toy log pieces? Well, making your adult log house involves the same principles: notching and fitting and joining. Variations in how you do it—always properly, I hope—are what produce the individual character that is so pleasing in log homes.

You have secured logs and peeled them; now, using a chain saw or ax, you are going to make alterations that will provide closer fitting, better utilization of materials, and, most important, sound construction.

Log Shaping

The standard round logs, those that are not shaped, have some disadvantages. They are very hard to chink, because there is little contact area between the logs. Thus weather protection is always a problem—essentially there is no weather seal. Round logs are also somewhat difficult to fit together at corners, where they must be joined properly to create a sturdy house or cabin.

19. *Another example of corner joinery; here the logs are cupped to accept companion logs and provide a tight seal.* (PHOTOGRAPH BY MATTHEW BARR)

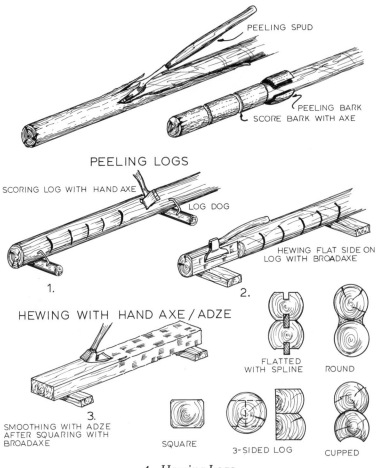

PEELING SPUD

PEELING BARK
SCORE BARK WITH AXE

PEELING LOGS

SCORING LOG WITH HAND AXE

LOG DOG

HEWING FLAT SIDE ON
LOG WITH BROADAXE

1.

2.

HEWING WITH HAND AXE / ADZE

3.
SMOOTHING WITH ADZE
AFTER SQUARING WITH
BROADAXE

FLATTED
WITH SPLINE

ROUND

SQUARE

3-SIDED LOG

CUPPED

4. *Hewing Logs*

FLATTENED LOGS

Flattened logs are much easier to work with than round ones. To flatten a round log, slice (saw) a slab off opposite sides. This simple sawing permits a tight fit between the logs for insulation, provides a wide area at the joints where logs cross and meet each other, and makes the logs uniform in thickness—an advantage not only for walls but also for level areas for windows and doors and for rooflines.

Logs can be flat on one side, or two sides, or on three sides, depending on how much time you have and, more important, on the design of the house itself. Generally, the one-side- flattened log works very well in construction.

THREE-SIDED LOGS

Three-sided logs create a flat and uniform inside wall, and with them you can use larger logs, further increasing the good looks. Good joints are vital for good log construction, so it pays to practice and take the time to learn how to cut and work with three-sided logs. Here is where the woodcrafter's art takes hold, and making the various joints can be fun because it is creative.

CUPPED LOGS

Removing a section of a log and making a cupped indentation takes time, but it ensures a tight fit. The bottom of each log is hollowed out with a gutter adze; each log thus fits snugly into the next log. The joint requires shaping only on one side of each log and allows the logs to shed water.

Instead of a cupped indentation, you can make a V-shaped groove on each log, using a chainsaw, though the joint will not be as tight as a carefully made cupped joint.

SPLINE CUTS

Logs that have been flattened on two or three sides are sometimes also splined together for increased strength and tightness. Kit homes generally use this spline construction. You can do it on your own, but spline cuts are difficult to make. Run a straight, uniform groove about 1 inch wide and 2 inches deep into the top and bottom of each log. Then insert a spline (a board) to form the union.

20. *These logs are not caulked, but the seal seems secure nonetheless.* (PHOTOGRAPH BY MATTHEW BARR)

Extended Corner Joints

We have briefly discussed the several log shapes you can use in constructing your log house; equally important are the joints where the logs fit together. You can use a saddle notch joint, a tenon notch, a dovetail notch, and so forth. They are much like the joints in basic furniture carpentry. Let us first look at extended corners.

SADDLE (SINGLE) NOTCH

This is a fairly easy joint to make with hand tools; the cut is made on the bottom only of each log, halfway through. No spikes are needed for joining.

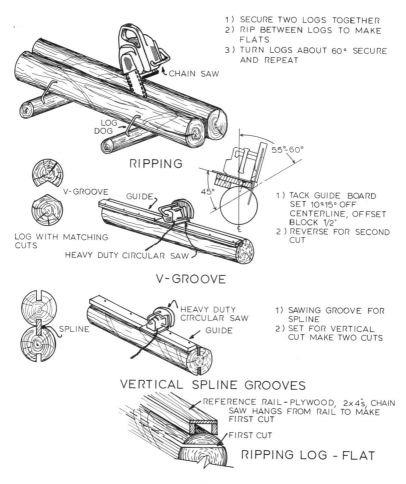

1) SECURE TWO LOGS TOGETHER
2) RIP BETWEEN LOGS TO MAKE FLATS
3) TURN LOGS ABOUT 60° SECURE AND REPEAT

CHAIN SAW

LOG DOG

RIPPING

55°-60°

45°

V-GROOVE

GUIDE

1) TACK GUIDE BOARD SET 10°-15° OFF CENTERLINE, OFFSET BLOCK 1/2"
2) REVERSE FOR SECOND CUT

LOG WITH MATCHING CUTS

HEAVY DUTY CIRCULAR SAW

V-GROOVE

SPLINE

HEAVY DUTY CIRCULAR SAW

GUIDE

1) SAWING GROOVE FOR SPLINE
2) SET FOR VERTICAL CUT MAKE TWO CUTS

VERTICAL SPLINE GROOVES

REFERENCE RAIL - PLYWOOD, 2x4's, CHAIN SAW HANGS FROM RAIL TO MAKE FIRST CUT

FIRST CUT

RIPPING LOG - FLAT

4a. Working Logs

[43]

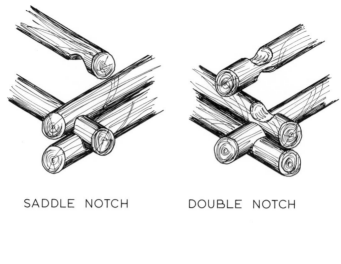

SADDLE NOTCH   DOUBLE NOTCH

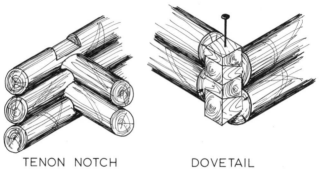

TENON NOTCH   DOVETAIL

5. *Corner Joints*

COMMON DOVETAIL

This is a handsome joint; the end of each log is notched out, leaving a wedge-shaped (fishtail or dovetail) section. When the other logs are similarly notched and joined, a tight union is formed.

TENON (DOUBLE) NOTCHES

These notches are based upon the carpenter's tenon joint. In the tenon notch, each log is cut on the top and bottom to about one-fourth its depth, and the wood is then removed. The logs fit together perfectly. In the double notch, the notch is cupped; this joint is easier to make with hand tools than the tenon notch, and the results are similar.

V-JOINT CORNER

There are several variations of this notch. Basically, the end of one log is cut to a V shape, which fits into a matching V groove on the side of another log. The joint requires spiking.

Flush Corner Joints

Some people prefer the flush look at the corners of the house because it creates a more finished appearance, less rustic than extended corners.

SADDLE END NOTCH

The notch is cut lengthwise, about 20 inches, one-fourth the depth of the log. This is similar to the saddle notch.

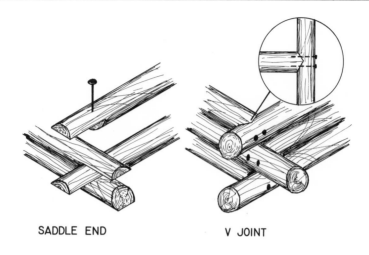

SADDLE END   V JOINT

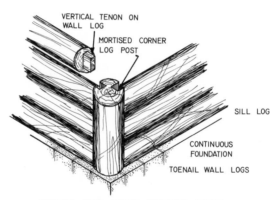

VERTICAL TENON ON
WALL LOG

MORTISED CORNER
LOG POST

SILL LOG

CONTINUOUS
FOUNDATION

TOENAIL WALL LOGS

TENON END WITH CORNER POST

6. Corner Joints

CORNER POST

Here the logs are squared at the end, and a log with perpendicular flattened sides is used in the vertical position. The logs are secured with bolts.

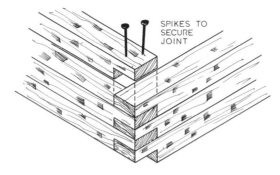

LAP OR RABBET JOINT

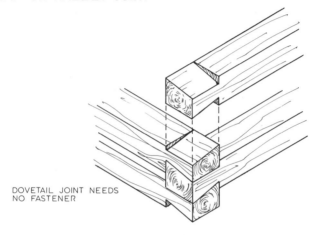

DOVETAIL JOINT

7. *Square Log Corner Joints*

TENON ENDS WITH POST

This is a difficult joint to make. One log is toenailed vertically and has a continuous groove cut away on two sides to accept logs that have tenons in each of their ends.

Joints for square-edged logs generally follow the same notching as the others described, with the square notch and dovetail notch being the most popular. With joints that fit securely, no bolts are needed, but still, the addition of spikes at the corners to hold the logs in position makes good sense. Use 80d or 100d galvanized spikes.

[47]

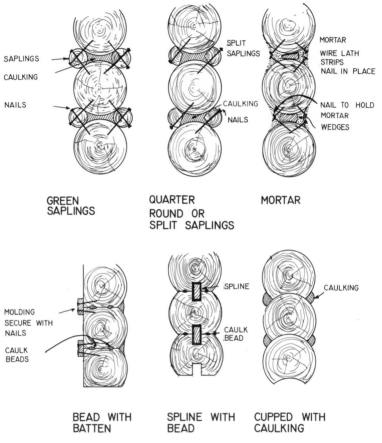

SAPLINGS

CAULKING

NAILS

GREEN
SAPLINGS

SPLIT
SAPLINGS

CAULKING

NAILS

QUARTER
ROUND OR
SPLIT SAPLINGS

MORTAR

WIRE LATH
STRIPS
NAIL IN PLACE

NAIL TO HOLD
MORTAR
WEDGES

MORTAR

MOLDING
SECURE WITH
NAILS

CAULK
BEADS

BEAD WITH
BATTEN

SPLINE

CAULK
BEAD

SPLINE WITH
BEAD

CAULKING

CUPPED WITH
CAULKING

NOTE : CAULKING - CLAY, MORTAR, FIBERGLASS OR
ANY EQUAL SEALANT

8. Caulking/Chinking

Chinking, Caulking, Sealing

Whatever you call it, chinking, caulking, or sealing involves making the log house weathertight by applying a material or materials to fit between the logs. Gaps must be filled or you forever will be sorry because of the constant maintenance required. Weatherproofing is a time-

21. *The property is overgrown but this log house is solid and sturdy; it is chinked with mortar.* (PHOTOGRAPH BY MATTHEW BARR)

22. *In this log construction the seal is a caulking compound.*
(PHOTOGRAPH BY MATTHEW BARR)

consuming but necessary job. It can be done several ways with several different materials. Just which you choose depends upon your own situation: what is available, how much time you have, and whether you have used round logs, flat logs, splines, etc. Let us look at the various materials used for chinking.

The most natural way to finish a log house and seal it tight is with strips of wood or pole quarter-rounds. Cedar or other split wood strips can be applied quickly, but unfortunately the chinking material is neither rodentproof nor waterproof. Saplings—whole or split—can also be used, and this is the traditional method, especially for round log joints. The strips of wood or saplings are applied between the joints and can be shaved to evenness.

Mortar chinking is favored by many builders and is a good sealant, except that it can crack as it dries. However, if applied in a semisolid—mudlike—consistency it works well, although it is not as attractive as the wood-sealed house. Oakum is a hemp-impregnated tar sometimes used to caulk the seams of log houses; it expands when damp, thus filling the joints, and it can be hammered tightly into place. It is then generally covered with some other material, such as strips or saplings.

Sphagnum moss is also used to caulk log houses. It is a poor sealant, but it is inexpensive and looks good.

Fiberglass is another insulation material used in chinking. It is covered with some other material, such as quarter-rounds and polyurethane foam, which must be painted or stained.

With flattened logs there are additional ways of sealing or chinking. Flattened logs will by nature fit quite tightly; so a simple lath stripping can be used over the logs. Mortar can also be applied between the logs, and a puttylike foam plastic sold in rope form is excellent for sealing logs. This is stapled in place and provides an almost airtight seal.

[51]

6

TOOLS AND HARDWARE

As with any building project, whether it be laying bricks or building a fence, there are certain tools you need. Axes, adzes, and chisels are vital when working with logs. In addition to these special log-building tools, you will also need standard tools, such as saws, hammers, and drills. And it is wise to have all tools on hand, because there is nothing more frustrating than having to continually run and chase around for tools. Hardware too is needed and should be in readiness. In this chapter we discuss all these items.

Ax

The ax, vital to log-house building, is a versatile tool that, if necessary, can do many jobs. The small double-bitted ax (about 28 inches) is necessary for working in tight places. A somewhat heavier and longer ax is necessary for notching. Keep two axes on hand—they are used so much in log construction—and be sure they are sharp. Frequently check the handle for cracks and the head for looseness. Know how to sharpen the ax yourself, and keep some shims (wedges of wood) on hand to keep the ax head tightly in place.

Hatchet

The hatchet—almost a forgotten tool—is important in log building because you can use it in a tight corner or at an awkward angle. Like the ax, it is a tool you must practice with to get the hang of it.

Adze and Broadax

The adze and broadax are tools used to flatten a portion of a log. These tools are not essential because you can use a chainsaw or the ax, but they do come in handy and are easier to use than the saw, for example.

Scribe

The scribe is a vital measurement tool for building. With a scribe you mark notches on logs and determine how much of a log to cut off for tight fitting to another log. For marking notches you need scribes that will adjust to several widths. Get the best scribe you can afford. A faulty scribe mark on a log can cause havoc, so be sure the pencil or pen that is attached to the scribe marks on damp surfaces and marks well.

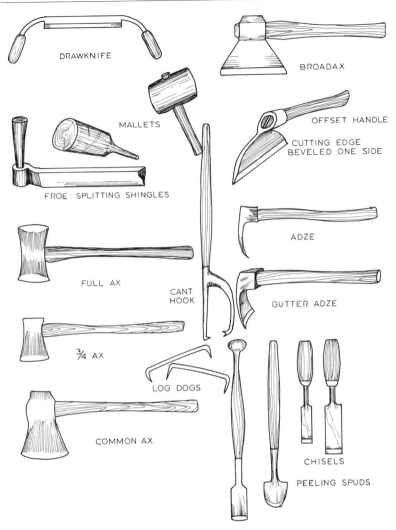

DRAWKNIFE

BROADAX

MALLETS

OFFSET HANDLE

CUTTING EDGE
BEVELED ONE SIDE

FROE SPLITTING SHINGLES

ADZE

FULL AX

CANT
HOOK

GUTTER ADZE

¾ AX

LOG DOGS

COMMON AX

CHISELS

PEELING SPUDS

9. Log Hand Tools

Drawknife and Peeling Spud

These tools are used to strip bark from logs; the blades should be at least 8 inches wide. The drawknife is used so much you might want two on hand. The peeling spud is also used for peeling logs, but may be hard to find, in which case the drawknife is sufficient.

Log Dog

Do not ask for this just anywhere, as people will think you are crazy. This is a tool used to hold logs in place while you work on them. It keeps the log in a temporary position. Select a country hardware store to find this, or if you cannot find one, make one from ⅝-inch metal rod. The dog should be about 30 inches long.

Chisels and Mallet

Chisels are essential in log work for notching wood evenly after you have made the saw cuts. Some chisels are for heavy chopping; others are for the fine paring necessary in finishing work. Chisels come in different lengths and widths, and the handles can be wood, plastic, or leather. Buy the best chisel you can afford. Chisels are not difficult to use, but they do require some expertise. You will need a wooden mallet to work a chisel with. Heavy wood mallets are available in different styles and sizes and are indispensable for chisel work.

An ordinary bench chisel (firmer chisel) is strong and can do heavy work. This chisel has a wooden or plastic handle and is made of carbon steel. A mortise chisel is somewhat heavy but very useful for mortise cutting. A smaller version of the mortise chisel, less heavy and easier to work with, is the sash mortise chisel.

The bevel-edge chisel is used for fine paring work, such as making acute angles or carving dovetails. This chisel is lightweight and thin and comes with short or long stocks. This is a very valuable log tool.

SHARPENING CHISELS

Periodically chisels must be sharpened. Hold the end to be sharpened at a 30-degree angle. Remember that the lower the angle of a chisel, the sharper the chisel will be, and thus it will cut more easily. Hold the chisel with the bevel flat on the oilstone (oilstones are sold at hardware stores). Stroke the tool back and forth on the stone with an even pressure. Hold the blade of the tool with one hand as you sharpen it, to steady it. Like using the chisel, sharpening takes some experience, but it's not difficult.

Planes

You will need a plane to remove unwanted portions of wood from a log. Unlike a chisel, a plane lets you control the depth and width of the cut. The bench and block planes are used for general carpentry.

The block plane is small, can be manipulated with one hand, and is used for smoothing with the grain along a board's length. Bench planes come in three sizes: the jointer plane, the jack plane, and the smooth plane. A long plane is best because it holds a straighter line; short ones have a tendency to ride up and down. The jack plane is the best for our work and measures from 12 to 15 inches long.

It is important to know exactly how to use a plane or you will ruin the wood with it. Sight down the plane's underside, and be sure the blade edge is protruding only slightly through the opening and is perfectly square across. If it is not, adjust it with the screw cap until it is. Angle the bench plane to get a shearing cut, and always cut in the

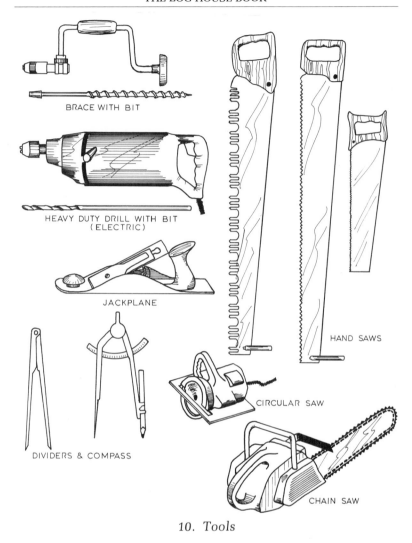

BRACE WITH BIT

HEAVY DUTY DRILL WITH BIT
(ELECTRIC)

JACKPLANE

DIVIDERS & COMPASS

HAND SAWS

CIRCULAR SAW

CHAIN SAW

10. *Tools*

same direction as the grain of the wood. Keep the cuts shallow but always even. Use more pressure at the front knob, and plane in short even strokes.

Saws

The saw is the universal cutting tool; you can use reliable handsaws or the more convenient and faster power saws. The basic handsaw used in carpentry is the crosscut saw. The power saws are the saber saw, band saw, circular saw, and continuous band saw. Handsaw lengths vary from 12 to 26 inches. A coarse tooth is better on thicker and softer woods; a fine tooth gives a cleaner edge. Also, a narrow blade cuts tighter curves than a wide blade.

CHAIN SAWS

The chain saw is perhaps the most valuable one for the log house builder; if you know how to use one properly, it is almost a portable sawmill. The chain saw makes it possible to square timbers from logs quickly and efficiently.

If you want to make boards or planks from logs with a chain saw, lay out the cut on the small end of the log; saw off the slabs on four sides to straighten the log. Then you can cut uniform boards from end to end. If you want to make a single flat surface on one log, the chain saw again does the job quickly.

To make joists, rafters, and studs with a chain saw, lay out two logs on a sawhorse (hold the logs together with a log dog). Run the chain saw blade between them, and you can saw two flat surfaces at one time.

Chain saws come in various models and weights; they are, at first, not easy to use, and some practice is necessary to get the feel of the saw. You do not have to get a large chain saw: a saw with a 14-inch bar is fine for most work. Be sure you can handle the weight of the saw, because at times you may have to hold it with one hand. Like all tools, the saw should be kept sharpened or it will not saw straight.

HANDSAWS

The standard crosscut saw is the handsaw you will use the most. It is used for cutting across the grain and is narrower at the end than at the blade. It is good to have one around if a chain saw is not available, not accurate enough, or cannot reach far enough.

PORTABLE POWER SAWS

A power saw may cut with a circular blade, a continuous band, or a short stiff blade, as in a saber saw. The circular saw is for straight cuts; the continuous band and saber saws are for cutting curves, with the saber saw being preferred because it is not restricted by the size of the area between the blade and the support. A saber saw is highly recommended because it is basically a portable jigsaw; because the end of the blade is free, it can cut both enclosed and external curves. The saber saw blade is stiff but not long and works on an up-and-down motion. The band saw, used for cutting both irregular and straight shapes, comes with a choice of blades. (Various types of power saws are also available as table models.) The standard portable circular saw has a blade 6 to 8 inches in diameter.

TABLE POWER SAWS

The basic table or bench saw is the circular saw, which is used for straight-line cutting, crosscutting, and ripping long boards. By tilting the blade you can achieve bevel cuts of any angle to 45 degrees. The saw has a sturdy table and an arbor and motor; the blade is secured to the arbor and driven by a motor with belts and pulleys. There are numerous circular saw blades, from crosscut to ripsaw. The depth of the cut is adjusted by the small table the saw projects through; this enables you to see ahead the line you are cutting.

The radial-arm saw does basically everything the circular saw does but has the extra advantage of being easy to use because it cuts from above the work. Layout marks are always in view on top of the wood. The saw remains stationary while the saw blade is moved over the work. The saw has a yoke-mounted motor suspended from a horizontal arm—the arm is mounted on a sturdy column at the rear. The motor, yoke, and horizontal arm can be adjusted to any desired angle. With various accessories the radial arm saw can grind, sand, shape, and rout.

The band saw makes bevel cuts up to 45 degrees. With this saw you can easily do compound cutting and pattern sawing. The blade is made of flexible steel, with the ends welded together to form a continuous band. The blade is set over two large wheels; the size of the band saw is measured by the wheel diameter.

Drills and Bits

You can use an old-fashioned hand drill, but the power drill is easier to use and far superior. The most common electric drill takes drills up to ¼ inch in diameter. These trigger-type drills operate on standard household current. With a power hand drill you essentially have many tools in one, because you can use a variety of attachments to make the drill a sander or a saber saw, for example. Check local hardware stores for drill attachments.

Larger holes can be made with power bits, which look something like a chisel with a sharp barb in the middle of the blade. Or you can use an old-fashioned brace and bit. For extra-long holes in thick logs, you will need a bit extender.

Miscellaneous Tools

You will need, as in all construction, a tape measure—select a good one, at least 50 feet long—and a level—costly but necessary unless you have a really keen eye, and who has? Buy a 36-inch level. Get a carpenter's square if you do not already have one, and a chalk line. A punch is handy to drive spikes into predrilled holes, and a vise is needed to hold materials. For making 45-degree cuts in small pieces of wood—door and window frames, for example—a miter box is handy, and wrenches and screwdrivers are all part of the carpentry toolbox.

And, yes, you will need ladders—a short sturdy one and a long 18-foot one. Also keep on hand some chain and rope for hauling and moving logs and for assorted other chores.

Nails, Bolts, and Screws

It is essential to know a little something about nails, bolts, and other fasteners when you work with wood. There are finishing nails, common nails, roofing nails, and so forth, and it is best to use the right nail for the right place. Spikes and bolts are also important in wood construction, and these too come in an assortment of sizes and lengths. Here is a short course on hardware.

Nails can be purchased by bulk weight by the pound or in plastic boxes. Most nails are available in sizes from 2 to 20 penny (denoted by the initial d). At one time the penny meant the price of 100 hand-forged nails, but not so now; today it means the length of the nail, from 1 inch (2d) to 4 inches (20d).

Common or box nails are used for most construction and for joining headers to joists, joists to sills and girders, and so on. An assortment of 8d, 12d, and 16d nails should take care of most of your construction. Use finishing nails for interior work, such as moldings. These come in 3d (1¼ inches) to 10d (3 inches). And for corner joints and joist connections you will probably need spikes and bolts. The size of the spike is dictated by the logs used. Hardware stores sell suitable spikes.

Various screws are used in roof construction and for fastening dimensional lumber. Lag screws are very large wood screws with a square head; they are tightened with a wrench. Self-tapping screws are used for sheet-metal work, mainly flashings. They come in various sizes. Dowel screws are used for invisible fastening.

Machine bolts are available with several different types of heads. These are called screws but really are bolts. Carriage bolts are large, with a square collar under the head that sinks into the wood. A nut is used to keep it in place.

Foundation bolts are used for bolting wood or metal to concrete. The head is set in wet concrete; the bolt holds firmly when the concrete dries. They are sometimes called anchor bolts.

7

FOUNDATIONS AND FOOTINGS

You could set your log house directly on the ground, but of course within a short time the logs would rot, and all the work you put into the building would be wasted. A house is only as good as its foundation. The foundation must support the house, hold it straight, and create a base.

In standard construction the continuous foundation of concrete is frequently used because it is solid and supports the weight of the structure well. However, this is a tough job to do yourself and is best done by professionals (our drawing shows a continuous concrete foundation wall). A footing and foundation wall of concrete block is easier for the beginner and quite satisfactory, so let's look at this installation.

The Concrete Footing and Block Wall

A continuous concrete footing and foundation wall is just what it implies: The footing is concrete, and the foundation, poured after the footings have set, is also concrete. As previously mentioned, footings can be used with concrete block as the foundation wall. Designs vary, depending upon the building codes of different areas, but the following general plan can be used for footing work:

1. Drive twelve stakes or four batten boards (short boards) 4 to 8 feet from the proposed corners. Lay out the exact plan of the building with string from stake to stake or board to board.
2. Dig a trench approximately 2 feet wide and a minimum of 1 foot deep (or whatever building codes advise) around the perimeter of the proposed site.
3. Decide what height the foundation footing will be, and then use a level to make sure all batten boards or stakes are on the same level.
4. Rent foundation framing equipment, or use ¾-inch

23. A concrete-block foundation is shown here; the floor is cement. (PHOTOGRAPH BY MATTHEW BARR)

24. *The log house with a stone foundation—a nice harmony of stone and wood.* (PHOTOGRAPH BY MATTHEW BARR)

plywood. The width of the footing should be 8 inches or whatever local building codes require.

5. Reinforce footings with steel rods inlaid horizontally and vertically. Pound the vertical rods into the ground between the foundation framing and then tie the horizontal rods (use wires) to the vertical ones. Use a standard concrete mixture and fill forms.

6. After footings have set—24 to 48 hours—strip off forms.

25. *Closeup of stone foundation wall.* (PHOTOGRAPH BY MATTHEW BARR)

26. *Rock and logs make up this structure; the foundation is the same as the walls.* (PHOTOGRAPH BY MATTHEW BARR)

27. Forms readied for a concrete pour for footings and foundations. (PHOTOGRAPH BY MATTHEW BARR)

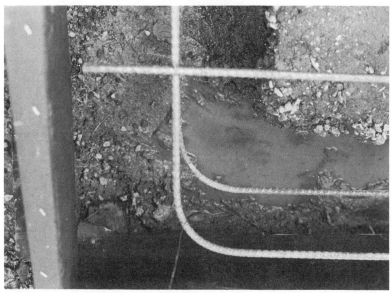

28. Rebar installed in a footing trench; the next step is the pouring of concrete. (PHOTOGRAPH BY MATTHEW BARR)

Concrete Blocks

To build a concrete-block foundation wall, strip away the concrete forms used for the footings. Start by laying down a bed of mortar in the middle of the concrete footing, beginning at a corner and for several block lengths. Use a plumb bob to locate the first block, set it in place, and tap it down gently with a hammer. Add globs of mortar to the outside and inside edges of that block, and then set the next block in line at the same level. Keep installing blocks, but as you go along check with a level to be sure all is properly done. Keep blocks uniformly spaced, and stagger the blocks on successive rows. Use a somewhat stiff mortar, because

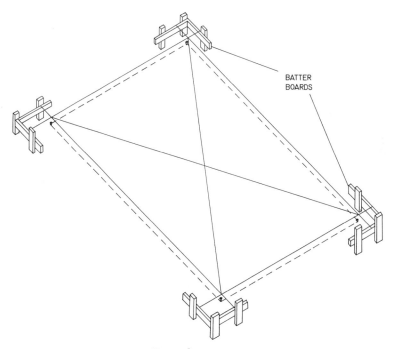

BATTER
BOARDS

11. Foundation Layout

you do not want mortar running all over. The mortar bed should be about ⅜ inch thick. As you install the blocks, remember to leave space for a cellar window or at least air vents.

Standard steel rebars prevent frost heaving. Periodically insert these bars down through the voids in the blocks, and cement them in place with generous amounts of mortar. At the top of the last course of blocks, put in a ½-inch bolt 12 inches long every 6 to 8 feet, with the bolt head set down in mortar; leave about 8 inches of the rest of the bolt exposed. On top of these bolts install the sill logs. Where local conditions dictate, install termite shields wherever wood and concrete meet; metal flashing is suitable.

29. This is a pier installation using concrete columns for a foundation of a log house. (PHOTOGRAPH BY MATTHEW BARR)

30. Here log poles are used to hold up a house and act as foundation posts; they are sunk in concrete. (PHOTOGRAPH BY MATTHEW BARR)

Pier Installation

If you do not want storage space under the house, or if there is bedrock on the site that would make building a foundation very difficult, you might want to use piers to support the house. This is an inexpensive way of building, but in very cold climates you will then have to insulate and seal the underside of the house for any comfort in winter.

Lay out the foundation plan as described for continuous foundations. When you get the building square, adjust corner stakes and put them in the ground firmly. Place the stakes to mark piers in the ground.

Just how many piers you install depends upon the length

of logs used, but generally a 10-foot span is good. Dig holes for the piers; place each pier on a concrete pad. The concrete conforms to the bottom of the hole and levels easily. While the concrete pad is wet you can install rebars to bond the piers to the pad. Dig holes for piers at least 24 inches wide; the depth depends upon the frost line. (Call local building office to get frost line in your area.)

After you have dug the holes and installed the concrete with short pieces of rebar, set the piers. Plumb each pier while tamping a few inches of earth at the bottom of the hole to hold the pier in place vertically. Prop the piers with scrap lumber with appropriate box braces.

Lumberyards sell a variety of piers, and many are suitable for foundation work if you reside in temperate climates. One pier I have used is a concrete collar and nailing block; another has a concrete collar and an imbedded post anchored with a drift pin.

Sonotubes

Sonotube installation is somewhat different but easier than piers. A sonotube is a cardboard column you fill with concrete. Dig the holes as for pier construction but make them wide enough for the columns. Set columns in place. Fill the sonotubes with concrete, and then insert a rebar down the middle until it hits the concrete at the bottom. When the concrete is almost stiff, insert a ⅝-inch bolt 12 inches long into the top of the pier in the outer rows. Leave at least 8 inches of the bolt exposed vertically so you can fasten down the logs to the piers.

As you pour the concrete into the tubes, tap down with a stick to eliminate air bubbles; tap the outside with a hammer to drive away any pebbles from the surface of the concrete, to be sure of a smooth, unbroken surface at the top of the pier.

In average temperatures of 45 to 75 degrees you can peel off the cardboard in forty-eight hours, but in cooler

31. *Sonotube piers are the main foundation of this structure.*
(PHOTOGRAPH BY MATTHEW BARR)

weather wait at least six days. In hot sunny weather wet the tubes periodically to cure the concrete and keep the tubes cool. If there is frost at night, protect the piers with tarps or hay covering to prevent freezing and thawing, which causes cracks.

Help?

Foundations and footings require precise layout and arduous digging so the site is level. Setting up forms and pouring concrete is no joke either and requires at least two people (three is better) on the job. If you do not have helping hands about, it might be best to let out the foundation work to a professional. Just how you tackle it, of course, depends on the size of your house.

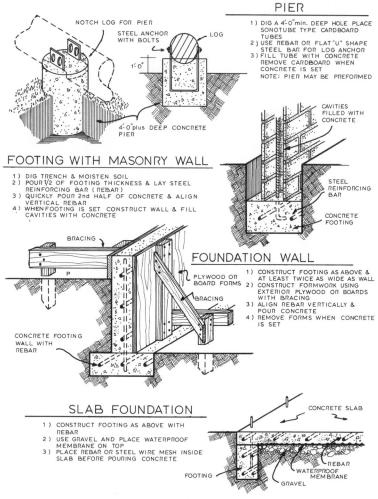

PIER

1) DIG A 4'-0"min. DEEP HOLE PLACE SONOTUBE TYPE CARDBOARD TUBES
2) USE REBAR OR FLAT "U" SHAPE STEEL BAR FOR LOG ANCHOR
3) FILL TUBE WITH CONCRETE REMOVE CARDBOARD WHEN CONCRETE IS SET
NOTE: PIER MAY BE PREFORMED

NOTCH LOG FOR PIER
STEEL ANCHOR WITH BOLTS
LOG
1'-0"
4'-0"plus DEEP CONCRETE PIER

CAVITIES FILLED WITH CONCRETE
STEEL REINFORCING BAR
CONCRETE FOOTING

FOOTING WITH MASONRY WALL

1) DIG TRENCH & MOISTEN SOIL
2) POUR 1/2 OF FOOTING THICKNESS & LAY STEEL REINFORCING BAR (REBAR)
3) QUICKLY POUR 2nd HALF OF CONCRETE & ALIGN VERTICAL REBAR
4) WHEN FOOTING IS SET CONSTRUCT WALL & FILL CAVITIES WITH CONCRETE

BRACING
P
PLYWOOD OR BOARD FORMS
BRACING
CONCRETE FOOTING WALL WITH REBAR

FOUNDATION WALL

1) CONSTRUCT FOOTING AS ABOVE & AT LEAST TWICE AS WIDE AS WALL
2) CONSTRUCT FORMWORK USING EXTERIOR PLYWOOD OR BOARDS WITH BRACING
3) ALIGN REBAR VERTICALLY & POUR CONCRETE
4) REMOVE FORMS WHEN CONCRETE IS SET

SLAB FOUNDATION

1) CONSTRUCT FOOTING AS ABOVE WITH REBAR
2) USE GRAVEL AND PLACE WATERPROOF MEMBRANE ON TOP
3) PLACE REBAR OR STEEL WIRE MESH INSIDE SLAB BEFORE POURING CONCRETE

CONCRETE SLAB
REBAR
WATERPROOF MEMBRANE
FOOTING
GRAVEL

11a. Foundations, Footings

8

CONSTRUCTION

After the foundations are in place, it is time to start the log construction. If you have any carpentry skill, you should be able to tackle these jobs on your own. If you have only limited skill, then I suggest that you engage the help of a friend who has carpentry knowledge or someone familiar with building construction. It is not necessary to hire a carpenter or contractor. You can do it, novice or not, but you will need some minimal outside help.

Sill Logs

The sill logs are the first logs laid on the sill of the foundation wall. They support the walls and distribute the weight of the building uniformly. In most cases the sill log is flattened on one side to fit flush on the foundation wall and is secured with anchor bolts. In a continuous foundation these logs must also have a notch for center girders. You can also lap-joint logs and fit them together with spikes for a sill (much harder to do).

On top of the foundation wall, install a sill-seal compound so there is an airtight seal between the foundation wall and log sill. Fiberglass is good for sealing and comes in rolls (buy it at hardware stores). For a con-

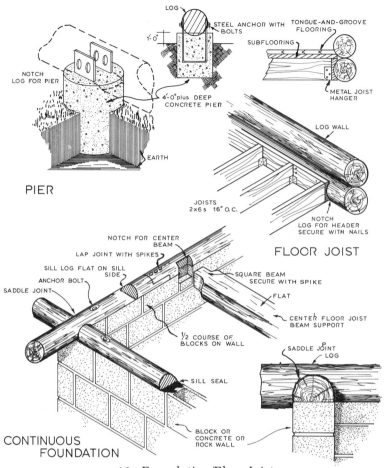

12. *Foundation/Floor Joist*

tinuous foundation the length of the log is not important—it can be spiked in at several points. Make the corner joints to the pattern you want (see Chapter 5), and then cut the logs to the final length. Mark the logs accurately to match the bolts in the foundation wall, and bore the holes at least ¼ inch larger than the anchor bolts; countersink for washers and nuts.

If you are doing pier installation, the sill logs must be flattened at the places directly over the piers. The flat sections must be parallel, so plan the sill-log placement carefully, because the logs must rest at specified points over the piers.

Floor Joists

Floor joists, usually 2 × 6 in standard construction, span the width of a room. Usually they are 16 inches apart on centers—that is, from the center of one joist edge to the

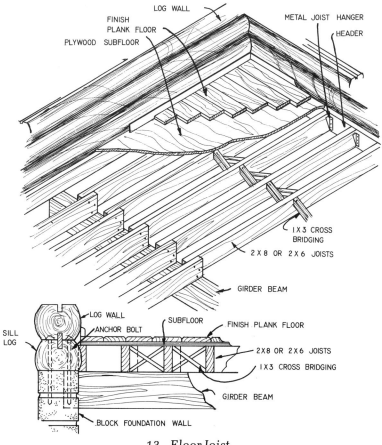

13. *Floor Joist*

32. Closeup of pier foundation; note leveled area for the house.
(PHOTOGRAPH BY BERNE HOLMAN)

center of the next. There are many ways of putting joists in place. Log joists, usually 24" apart on centers, may be saddle-notched onto sill beams and girders or nested into walls and girders. If you decide to use dimensional lumber (and this works very well), the best way is to box in the lumber, as in standard house construction. Nail a ledger to the sill log to support the end of the floor joists. The sill log should be flattened on the inside to accept the ledger. You can also notch the second log with a chain saw and chisel for each joist end. With these methods the floor will be at about the height of the second log.

Another simple way of installing a joist section is to use dimensional lumber boxed in as just discussed, with the header joists spiked into the sill log. Use metal joist hangers to hold the joists securely to the header.

Study and follow the working drawings of joist construction carefully, selecting the method that suits you.

Log Walls

To start the walls, first lay down plywood flooring over the joists you have installed. Use ⅝-inch plywood. Each log must be notched to take its position in the wall, so scribe for notching with a compass. You can use a saddle notch or whatever notch you want, but it must be done as explained: raised into position, scribed, and then lowered and notched. A chain saw and chisel do the work.

33. *The work site of the log house; note trees cut to make a clearing and wood neatly milled and stacked.* (PHOTOGRAPH BY BERNE HOLMAN)

[81]

34. *A two-storied gabled log house, homemade.* (PHOTOGRAPH BY MATTHEW BARR)

If logs will not span an entire wall (and frequently they do not), they must be spiked or doweled. Spikes must be long enough to reach through the log and several inches beyond. With some woods, like pine, you can hammer directly into the wood with the spikes, but for other woods, pilot holes must be drilled first.

Openings for windows and doors must be thought about before erecting complete walls; it is wise to use short logs between spans of windows and doors. Be sure sections are plumbed and aligned with other logs for proper fit.

If you cannot arrange to have short logs span window and door openings (that is, end where a door or window should be), then mark out windows and doors. Tack a 2 × 6 sawing guide in place vertically, and mark a niche in the log above the end of the 1 × 6 to accept a saw. Remember to cut windowsill logs at a slight angle for drainage.

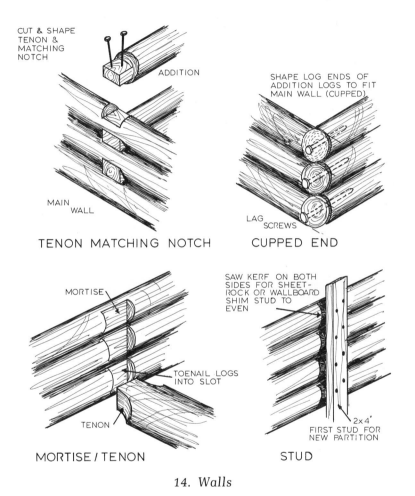

CUT & SHAPE TENON & MATCHING NOTCH

ADDITION

MAIN WALL

TENON MATCHING NOTCH

SHAPE LOG ENDS OF ADDITION LOGS TO FIT MAIN WALL (CUPPED)

LAG SCREWS

CUPPED END

MORTISE

TOENAIL LOGS INTO SLOT

TENON

MORTISE / TENON

SAW KERF ON BOTH SIDES FOR SHEET-ROCK OR WALLBOARD SHIM STUD TO EVEN

2x4"
FIRST STUD FOR NEW PARTITION

STUD

14. *Walls*

Vertical Log Walls

We generally think of log houses with logs placed horizontally, but you can also build with logs placed vertically for walls. In this situation there are no complex corner joints and you can use short logs, say 8 feet long.

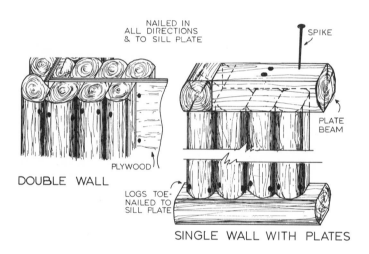

SPIKED AT TOP
TO PLATE

NAILED IN
ALL DIRECTIONS
& TO SILL PLATE

SPIKE

PLATE
BEAM

DOUBLE WALL

PLYWOOD

LOGS TOE-
NAILED TO
SILL PLATE

SINGLE WALL WITH PLATES

LOGS NAILED TO
PLYWOOD

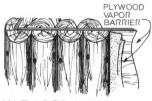

PLYWOOD
VAPOR
BARRIER

NOTE: CAULKING
TO BE USED
ALL WALLS

HALF LOGS WITH
PLYWOOD
DOUBLE WALL

15. Vertical Log Walls

This is sometimes called the stockade type of building and is as easy as the traditional log structure. Spikes are used to attach logs at top and bottom plates; plates are usually standard boards. Sealing the joints follows the same procedure as for horizontal construction: caulking or splines.

As shown in the drawing, there are several variations on the vertical-wall construction method: a double wall with plywood separating the logs, single logs, or half-logs with a plywood double wall.

Second Floor

Once the first-floor walls are installed it is time to put in joists for a second floor (if there is to be one). Joist spacing is usually on 30-inch centers, with 10 × 10-inch girders where load-bearing walls are to be built. Placing main girders over walls makes it easy to fit wallboard and paneling around the open log rafters.

To support the floor joists, make notches in the wall logs at the desired height. To make notches with a chain saw and chisel, you will need staging unless you have prenotched the logs before the wall went up. If the wall logs are flattened, then the notching for joists is easy; they can be cut the full depth of the log vertically. The joist then fits flush in the notch but rests upon the log underneath.

It is not easy to lift girders and logs; it takes several people. Use a log ramp, and haul up logs with rope. If you are working with flat logs, use a block and tackle.

Roof

The roof really imparts the mood or character to the house. The roof can be simple or ornate, formal or

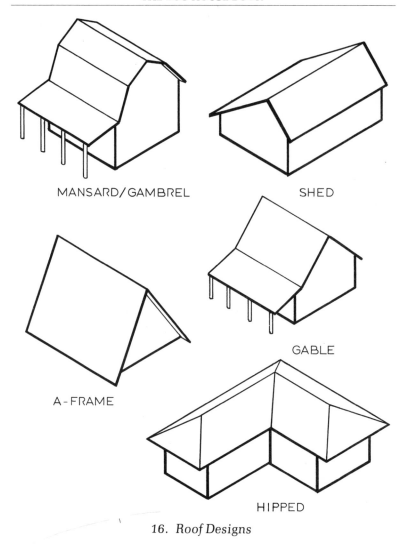

MANSARD/GAMBREL   SHED

A-FRAME

GABLE

HIPPED

16. Roof Designs

picturesque, utilitarian or decorative, or a little bit of each. Always remember that the underside of the roof is the ceiling of the house. Without a doubt, the more complex roofs—dormer, gabled, mansard—have the crafted touch; they look good and are in keeping with log construction.

The *pitched roof* has two slopes meeting at a ridge

parallel to a long axis of the building, and triangular gables at the ends. It is a popular roof style.

The *hipped* or *four-sloped roof* consists of slopes that should be equal to each other in pitch, forming hips or intersections bisected by corners and terminating with a ridge or apex at the top.

The *mansard roof* has all sides divided into two slopes, with the lower slope steeper than the upper: This is a decorative, ornate roof, quite effective. The *gambrel roof* is similar to the mansard but has gable ends; it is built the same way and it too is decorative and picturesque.

The *gabled roof,* popular and effective, offers easy construction and is basically triangular in shape. It provides attic space, and its construction involves both rafters and joists. All rafters are cut to the same length and pattern; each rafter is fastened at the top to a 2 × 6 ridge board.

In normal pitched-roof construction, joists are attached after both interior and exterior wall framing is completed. Once the ceiling joists are in, rafters are then erected. The rafters are cut and notched for the top plates. The studs for gable-end walls are nailed to the end rafter and the top plate of the end-wall sole plate.

RAFTERS AND BEAMS

The rafters and beams are the actual members that hold up the roof or the ceiling. A ceiling is the bottom side of an upstairs bedroom or the bottom of a roof. Exposing the joists and rafters, as is usually done in log homes, adds depth and height to a room and creates a much more interesting character than a flat surface would. Rafters and beams can support a roof in many different ways or designs, and how they are patterned should be considered if they are to be exposed.

The rafter rests on the last top log of a wall. The plate log can hold a rafter in three ways: (1) it can be notched for the rafter, (2) a wall tie beam can be used with the rafter, or (3) the plate log may be flattened to accept the rafter. Once the

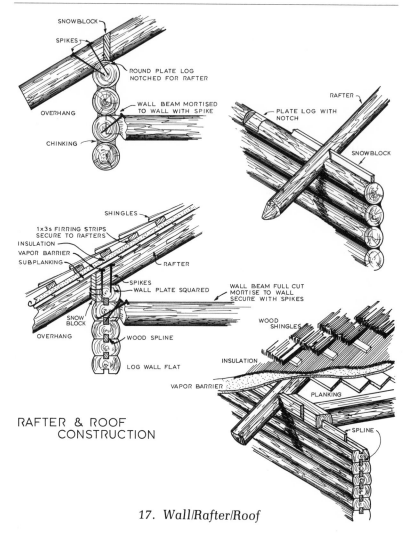

RAFTER & ROOF
CONSTRUCTION

17. Wall/Rafter/Roof

log gable ends are up, the rafters can be put in place. Rafters are joined with or without a ridgepole. The ridgepole method probably is stronger; in this case the rafter has to be spiked to the ridgepole.

Setting the snowblock in place first over the sill course will help you set the main rafters. Use two rafters as guides, and determine where the ridgepole ties into the peak of the gable end. Nail the ridgepole in place with 16d nails, and then temporarily brace the pole with 2 × 4s. Where two rafters meet will be the butt joint. Beginning at one gable end, lay out rafters, a pair at a time. Hold the rafters in place by toenailing them with 16d nails through the ridgepole. Set all rafters and spike them securely in place.

The continuous snowblock should now be in place between the rafters, which have been cut to fit the snowblock. Chisel notches on either side of the rafters so the snowblock fits securely over the sill course below. To provide an adequate weatherproof seal, use urethane foam or butyl caulking.

A type of roof construction that can be used in place of rafters or with them involves roof beams (called purlins) that run the length of the house and tie into the gable ends. The purlins carry the weight of the roof to the gable ends, and there is very little roof load on the sidewalls. Consequently there is no need for crosstie beams to keep the walls from spreading, as when rafters are used.

INSULATION FOR THE ROOF

An uninsulated roof protects your house from rain and snow, but wherever winters are cold, insulation is vital. The log house with no attic space has no dead-air space to help insulate the living spaces, so if your log home is for year-round, insulation is necessary. If you have used dimensional lumber for rafters, you can install insulation between the rafters. If you have used log rafters, build the roof with insulation upward from the rafters, because wallboard and paneling are difficult to fit between irregular rafters.

With round log rafters you can use ½-inch plywood sheathing nailed on 24-inch centers or tongue-and-groove roof sheathing. Over this, apply a vapor barrier to keep out moisture: Kraft paper, foil, or building felt is fine. It is now time to insulate. The amount of insulation depends upon your individual climate. Generally, fiberglass insulation is used. For more on insulation, see Chapter 10.

Roofing

Now that you have the roof framing in place—girders and rafters and snowblocks (where necessary)—it is time to select the roofing material. The type of "skin" you put on your roof can be asphalt shingles, wood shingles, or even aluminum shingles. Consider the style of the house; the roofing material should be appropriate to it. On sloping roofs, wood or asphalt shingles suit the feeling of the log house.

Remember also that the roof must protect the house from weather, be durable—you do not want to have to replace it every five years—and be fire-resistant. Asphalt and wood shingles have good water-shedding properties.

Asphalt shingles are inexpensive, easy to apply, and meet fire-protection codes. Wood shingles are just as easy to apply, but are expensive and may not meet your local fire codes. An asphalt roof can last as long as twenty years before replacement is necessary. Shingles come in different weights, shapes, and colors. A 235-pound weight of asphalt shingles refers to the weight of installed shingles per 100 square feet. Light-colored asphalt shingles reflect the heat better than dark-colored ones. Light colors make a building appear taller, whereas dark colors give a house a low profile.

Underlayment is required for roofing; this is usually roofing felt. The codes can get complicated in regards to roofing felts and which one to use. It depends upon whether you use double- or triple-covered shingles. Double-covered means there are two layers of shingles on each course. Triple-covered means there are three layers. Generally, underlayment is necessary, so figure on it. It is easily applied, inexpensive, and helps keep the roof in shape.

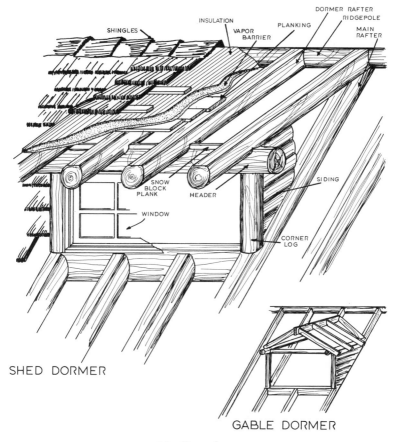

SHED DORMER

GABLE DORMER

18. Dormers

LAYING SHINGLES

An average asphalt shingle is 12 inches deep and 36 inches wide, with two slots dividing the shingle into three equal parts. Each end has a half-slot so that when the shingle butts against another shingle the two half-slots make a whole slot. To lay shingles (no matter what type you select), lay the first course topside toward the eave, and then lay a regular course right side up directly on top of it. Use galvanized roofing nails about 1 inch long. Drive four nails into each shingle. When installing the starter course, cut the first shingle in half. If you lay all the courses with full shingles, the joints lie over each other, which may allow leakage and looks bad.

Cut shingles with a shingle knife on the reverse side by cutting them *partially* and then snapping off the rest of the way. Lay the first course; then lay the second course, beginning with a half shingle, and then the third course, with a full shingle, and so on. This allows the slots of the shingles to alternate properly. When you get to the peak of the roof, cut shingles into thirds and fold them equally so each one goes over the ridge and overlaps 6 inches (to get double coverage). If the roof has valleys in it, you have to install flashing (discussed below). Where two parts of equal slope meet, fold the metal flashing so that equal widths extend away from the valley.

Flashing is always applied around joints and around chimney openings and vents. Use roofing cement to seal the edges between the flashing and the shingles. Plumbing vent pipes and roof vents come with their own flashing and are installed with the collar under the shingles—again, a generous amount of roofing cement is used.

Wood shingles are either redwood or cedar and edge-grained ,so there will be no curling. Wood looks handsome on log houses, so if you can afford it, it may be the answer. Wood shingles are usually 18 inches long and about ¼ inch thick at the butt, tapering to 1/32 inch. They are generally laid exposed 5 inches, but this depends upon the slope of the roof itself. A very popular kind of shingle is called a "shake," which is a shingle that is hand-split on the exposed side and sawed on the bottom side. Shakes come in lengths of 18 and 24 inches and can be exposed 7 to 10 inches—again, depending upon the slope of the roof.

An underlayment is not necessary for wood shingles; however, it is for the shakes, and the preparation is much the same as for asphalt shingles.

Double the first course of wood shingles and install them so they extend ½ inch beyond the eaves. Use two wood-shingle nails for each shingle and 3d or 4d galvanized nails. Then install plywood sheathing or furring strips with ring-shanked nails. Space nails ¾ inch from each edge and 1½ inches from the nails in the course below.

For shakes, use longer galvanized nails. Place an underlayment (usually a 20-pound felt) underneath each course of shakes. Use a strip of felt under the starter course and under the first course at the edge of the eave. Put in another strip of felt about halfway up the shake so that its bottom edge is well underneath the butt of the next course. Treat valleys as you would with asphalt shingles.

Most roofs need a metal drip edge that fits along the eave and rake of the roof and sticks out over the fascia (roof-edge trim) to allow water to drip away from the house. The metal edge (a folded piece of aluminum) also provides a good nailing base for the shingles themselves. Some houses will also need gutters and downspouts.

FLASHING

Flashing is a word that scares most amateur builders but it is only sheet metal or asphalt roll roofing formed to seal unions and junctures of the roof structure. For example, flashing is used where chimneys protrude from the roof, in valleys of the roof, and for dormer windows. Flashing is also necessary along gutter and eaves. The purpose of flashing is to create a tight seal and eliminate any leaks; thus it is an important part of building. It is simple to install. Form the flashing to fit the juncture after cutting it from the metal or roll roofing and nail it securely in place. Metal flashing may be aluminum, copper (the best), or galvanized steel.

Flashing for roof valleys should be about 20-inch wide rectangular pieces. For dormer windows the flashing should be L-shaped. Roll roofing works well in these areas.

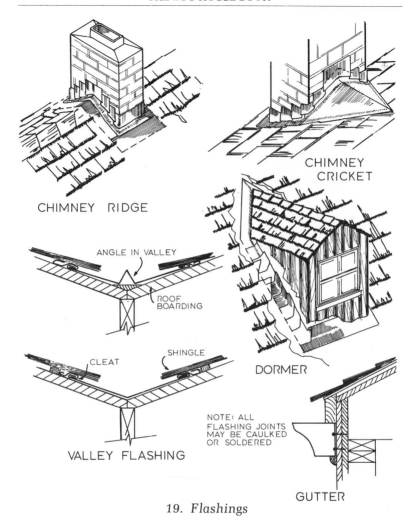

CHIMNEY RIDGE

CHIMNEY CRICKET

ANGLE IN VALLEY

ROOF BOARDING

CLEAT

SHINGLE

DORMER

VALLEY FLASHING

NOTE: ALL FLASHING JOINTS MAY BE CAULKED OR SOLDERED

GUTTER

19. Flashings

Floors

Floors are very important to the total impression of a house, depending upon whether they are barren expanses of concrete (hardly aesthetic), carpeted (the easy way out), or wood in various patterns. The crafted look is most apparent in a handsome wood floor; it adds character and beauty to any home. For example, the beauty of a parquet floor is immediately apparent because it adds design and dimension to a home. And the plank floor or standard hardwood floor is as handsome as any surfacing you can get.

The basic wooden floor construction is the same for most styles of wood floors; only the wood and the pattern differ. Essentially, wooden floors have joists, headers, bridging, subflooring, and the flooring material itself. The joists, discussed earlier in this chapter, are the floor skeleton and are 2 × 6s, 2 × 8s, or 2 × 10s placed on edge, usually on 12- or 16-inch centers. The width depends upon the span the joists must bridge.

The ends of the joists rest on supports—either a basement wall or a foundation. If the span is too great for a single joist, a girder is put down the middle of the span; then joists run from the walls on both sides to meet the girder. They are overlapped at this point. The girder is usually an 8 × 8 supported at the ends on the foundation, with a column or two to support the girder in the middle.

The floor must support walls, so the joists must have some support. Wherever there is a joist under a wall, the joist is doubled by spiking together new members. If a wall runs between joists, a bridging is used between the two joists the wall comes between. For bridging, use planks the same dimension as the joists and spike them in place with 20d spikes through both joists into the ends of the bridging. Bridging increases the rigidity of the floor by distributing stress up and down the joists laterally.

Where joists rest on basement walls or foundations, headers are used to hold them vertically. Hammer in 2-inch planks spiked across the ends of the joists. The header is nailed to the sill, which is the wooden member running along the top of the masonry wall.

Years ago the subfloor was the floor. Boards were nailed to joists; they were the floor. Today subfloors are plywood (not good for final surfacing), or individual boards laid on top of joists at a 45-degree angle, and the finish flooring goes on top. Board subfloors are nailed diagonally across the joists so that when flooring is placed on top, no joints coincide and there are no weak spots.

Board subflooring is nominally 1 inch thick by 4, 6, or 8 inches wide (which means actual measurements are almost ¾ inch thick and 3½, 5½, or 7½ inches wide). It can be square-edged or regular tongue-and-groove. You can apply subflooring boards perpendicular to the joists, instead of diagonally, but this will determine the direction the wood finish flooring takes. On a diagonally laid subflooring, finish flooring can be applied parallel with or perpendicular to joists, but on perpendicularly laid subflooring it has to be applied perpendicular to the subflooring, which means parallel to the joists. Be sure subflooring boards meet over joists unless end-matched tongue-and-groove boards are used. If you use such boards, stagger joints so that no two successive courses of boards have joints over the same between-joists space. Plywood subflooring comes in several sizes; the size is dictated by the joists' position and the type and direction of finish flooring being used.

WOOD FLOORS

Most finish floors are 2-inch oak or maple strips of random lengths. These floors are quite handsome and very durable. There are many variations of the strip-flooring design and concept. Wooden boards, say in 5- or 6-inch widths, are my choice for a distinctive flooring because the true beauty of the wood shows. There is natural depth and sheen. Like 2-inch strip flooring, wood boards are tongue-and-groove. Some of the boards are decorated with simulated pegged holes, making them even more attractive to some tastes.

Standard old-fashioned wood floors ran approximately 1 inch in thickness (the floors in my house are 1½ inches thick). Modern strip flooring and board flooring is usually

¾ inch thick. However, today thinner boards are available; they are installed with adhesives rather than nailed and are prefinished. Some are quite handsome. Another popular floor covering is tongue-and-groove subflooring; it looks natural and rustic, has knots and an irregular grain, and when stained can be very effective. It definitely adds a touch of character to any house.

For real log-cabin character the random-width board floor is very handsome, although you can use any flooring you like, depending upon your imagaination. For example, designs incorporated into some boards produce a parquet effect. If you want to create a deliberate contrast between a rustic exterior and a finished, sophisticated interior, parquet floors might be a good idea.

LAYING STRIP OR BOARD FLOORING

After subflooring has been put in, install as-phalt-impregnated paper (building paper) to inhibit noise and cold. Lay the paper perpendicular to the direction the strips will go down. Use a 3-inch overlap for the paper at the seams. Now, starting at one edge of the room, continue laying strips across the floor to the opposite end. Or start in the center (harder) and work first to one edge, then the other. Always nail the first row of strips about ½ inch from the wall; the baseboard and shoe molding will cover the gap.

It is vital that the first strip or board be absolutely straight and parallel to the wall or the line based at the room center. Remember that the entire floor is based on that first row. If you're starting at one edge rather than in the center, always let the tongue of the board lead toward the center of the room.

Always use special flooring nails; they are harder and slimmer than regular nails. These nails are spiral-shaped or ringed for extra holding power. Remember that the nails go into the V where the tongue meets the edge of the strip. Nail at a 45-degree angle.

Doors and Windows

The doors and windows for your log house should ideally be handcrafted and thus unique. But most people cannot find that great salvage door or that charming casement window, and most people simply cannot make a door; it takes skill. What I am saying is that although you craft your log home yourself, you probably will have to buy prefabricated doors and windows. Yes, this is more expensive than making your own, but there are commercially made doors and windows that are good-looking and will be appropriate for your home. (Especially with windows, buy wooden-framed ones, not those that are metal-framed.)

The door and window spaces can be made as the walls go up or cut in after the walls are in place. Fastening door and window frames to log walls requires some expertise; there are about six ways to do it, with the tongue-and-groove method perhaps the most practical. You can also use a 1 × 1 rail placed vertically on the logs' ends and a matching slot for a window frame, or just slap a 2 × 6 on the log ends.

SETTING STOCK WINDOWS

If you are installing windows as the walls go up, when you come to where the first window should be, place the window on top of the log and plumb it so it is level and even. Be sure the window is right side up, with the proper side facing outward. Brace the window with a 2 × 4 nailed to the top of the window. Cut a block of wood to fit horizontally between the two sides of the window about halfway up and continue to lay logs; check each course for dimensions and to be sure everything is even and level. Do not yet insulate around windows; leave that until the roof is in place. Then you can use foam or caulking. A continuous log above the window acts as a lintel. If there is a gap, do not

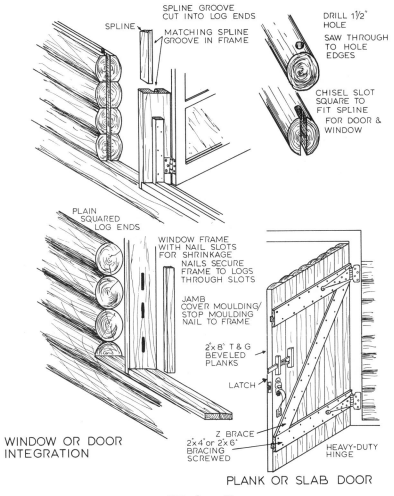

SPLINE

SPLINE GROOVE
CUT INTO LOG ENDS

MATCHING SPLINE
GROOVE IN FRAME

DRILL 1½"
HOLE

SAW THROUGH
TO HOLE
EDGES

CHISEL SLOT
SQUARE TO
FIT SPLINE
FOR DOOR &
WINDOW

PLAIN
SQUARED
LOG ENDS

WINDOW FRAME
WITH NAIL SLOTS
FOR SHRINKAGE

NAILS SECURE
FRAME TO LOGS
THROUGH SLOTS

JAMB
COVER MOULDING/
STOP MOULDING
NAIL TO FRAME

2"x 8" T & G
BEVELED
PLANKS

LATCH

Z BRACE
2"x 4" or 2"x 6"
BRACING
SCREWED

HEAVY-DUTY
HINGE

WINDOW OR DOOR
INTEGRATION

PLANK OR SLAB DOOR

20. Windows/Doors

worry: It can be filled in later with board and copper or galvanized-tin flashing.

When you are setting doors and windows, remember that you want a ¾-inch space over each window and door, to allow the logs to settle. Be sure windows are properly seated in the opening over the log under the window sill. Apply window head flashing. Then nail a 1 × 2 trim board across

35. *Wooden windows such as these suit the log house well.*
(PHOTOGRAPH BY MATTHEW BARR)

the top outside of the window or door frame header that fits under the flashing. Spike it in place. On the inside nail a piece of trim across the top inside face of window or door frame headers. When you are filling gaps over windows and doors, remember to use a flexible caulking compound; rigid compounds will bind when settling occurs.

DORMER WINDOWS

A dormer is a gabled extension of an attic space through a sloping roof to allow vertical window opening. It creates usable upstairs space. There are two types: the shed dormer and the gable dormer. Either adds a charming note to a log house and of course creates additional living area.

The shed dormer uses corner logs and lintel to create the extension from the roof line. Dormer rafters are then put in place and roofing applied to match existing roofing. The gable dormer is different in design; it is somewhat more difficult to construct than the shed type. Both types require rafter headers, as shown in the drawing.

INSTALLING DOORS

Putting a door in place or hanging it was once a complicated job, but not today. If proper stud framing exists, hanging the door should not take more than an hour. The prehung door frame is like a box with a door hinged to it. This lets you slip the box into a stud-framed opening and secure it easily. Each prehung frame has two side jambs and a head jamb dadoed together at the top. The doorstop or the molding runs around the inside of the jambs, and a sill and threshold are needed at the base of the two side jambs. The threshold closes the opening at the bottom of the door, and the sill slopes away from the door base to keep out water.

The frame usually comes with hinges attached and the doorstop molding tacked to the frame. Pull out the hinge pins and remove the door while attaching the frame in place.

If you build your own framing for a door, remember it must be absolutely plumb and level. Once the full-length studs are positioned, you can line up your trimmer studs' framing. Then install the header, usually a 4 × 4-inch piece of wood. Its length is the distance between the two existing full-length studs. Now figure the length of the trimmer studs; they extend from the floor to the base of the headers. Tack one trimmer against the inside of each full-length stud into the headers' ends, and toenail the cut-off full-length

36. *Window and door detail of a log house.* (PHOTOGRAPH BY MATTHEW BARR)

studs into the top of the header. Nail the outer trimmers into the studs.

To adjust the door frame to the proper width, put another trimmer out from one side parallel to the other trimmer stud and allow ½ inch on each side for shimming. Nail that trimmer into the block; toenail it to the sole plate and headers.

The door knob and lock should be placed 36 to 38 inches above the floor. Follow the manufacturer's directions for attaching the lock. After the doorknob is secured, mark the top and bottom of the latch where it hits the frame. Position the latch's striker plate, and cut out the mortise for the latch.

The finishing touches are the doorstop molding and

casing. Nail stops flush with the face of the closed door. Now nail casing trim around the opening to both the trimmer studs and the frame edges.

To hang a prehung frame in an opening, be sure the door frame is plumb and level at all times. The stud opening should be somewhat larger than the size of the prehung frame, to allow for shimming. To shim, drive a pair of shingles into the gap between the trimmer studs and the jamb to form a tight rectangular wedge. After the frame is nailed in place, cut off the shims flush with the studs.

To position the door, center the frame from side to side and back to front in the opening and then shim it to the estimated side clearance and fasten it. Cut shingles next to the upper hinge, and tap them together so the side of the jamb is plumb. Shim, check the plumb, and nail halfway between the top and bottom shims. Fasten the door into position with hinge pins, and shim and nail each side of the door frame, always keeping a 1/16-inch clearance between the door edge and frame. Nail doorsill and threshold in place.

If you want to make your own door, by all means try one. You can put together a handsome log panel door with 2 × 8-inch tongue-and-groove beveled planks joined with splines. Bracing of 2 × 6 planks is used to keep the door together and also acts as a decorative design. Then hinges and latches are put in place. Not easy but not impossible, and very handsome.

9

THE KIT HOME

There are so many advantages to a log house—durability, rustic character, energy-efficiency—that many manufacturers now offer what is called a kit log house, and in many designs. For people who want the log-house character and/or for those trying to save money over conventional construction (and the kit log house does cost less), the kit or knocked-down packaged home makes good sense. You get logs already peeled, seasoned, and precut, and construction is much faster. These manufacturers provide catalogs and other information (see List of Manufacturers at the back of the book).

What You Get

Log-house manufacturers generally furnish logs that are squared on at least two sides; this expedites assembly and makes it easier for the average person to do the construction. Also, the logs are of uniform size, generally 6 to 8 inches thick, and come tongue-and-grooved, ensuring a tight fit. The woods used vary with each manufacturer; white pine, white cedar, and spruce are typical.

Just as the logs are machine-precut, so are the joints, usually saddle or tenon. Caulking is furnished with the

37. An example of a Boyne log house—good design and nice structure. (COURTESY BOYNE LOG HOMES)

package; each log is caulked as it goes into place. The logs already have been treated with preservatives (another plus), and all necessary hardware, such as spikes and bolts, is included.

Detailed instructions for assembly are furnished, and logs are marked to key them to each section of the house. The log kit is very much like the commercially packaged greenhouse.

What you do *not* get is the foundation; this you must furnish. With most kit homes you also must furnish the floor joists and sometimes the sills (standard-type construction and lumber are recommended).

When you order your kit house you must take into account distance—that is, the location of the manufacturer and the location of your site. Trucking is, of course, extra, and depending on the distance, your cost can go up $500 or more. Whenever possible, it is wise to order from a manufacturer close to your location.

Getting Ready for the Kit House

As with any house, you will have to have your foundation ready, which means excavation, leveling, and the installation of piers, slab, or continuous foundation. The logs arrive stacked (at a prearranged date and time) in a huge trailer truck. Be sure you have your building site ready and know exactly where you want the logs stacked. Your contract with the manufacturer will state that they deliver

38. *Typical kit-type house design and site preparation.* (COURTESY BUILDING LOGS, INC.)

the logs as close as possible to the site, and that is it. If your road will not accommodate a 40-foot trailer—and winding ones will not—be prepared to bring up the logs another way. You may be able to get permission to use fire roads if you contact the proper authorities.

Inclement weather can cause havoc on a delivery day, so check with the manufacturer a day ahead of time if you think rain is a possibility. This way you can make other arrangements for delivery. I say this because it is extremely difficult to remove mud from freshly sawn logs. It can be done, but it takes a great deal of time. Ice is another problem; ice on logs must be scraped away before the construction can start, and that is a time-consuming job.

After the logs are stacked, cover them well—use heavy tarps or other appropriate protection.

39. One of the smaller Boyne houses offered by the company.
(COURTESY BOYNE LOG HOMES)

As mentioned, logs are numbered and coded to an instruction sheet, so stack each set of logs in the vicinity of where they will go into the actual building. For example, put all the logs marked A in one stack, B in another, and so on. Stack window and door units upright.

Construction

The building of the precut log house is not too different from the make-it-yourself house. You will need foundations, sills, and electrical power brought to the site. If you have planned accordingly, your pier or continuous foundation will already be installed. Most kit houses do not include log floor joists for the first level, so you must have dimensional-lumber sills and joists ready.

The floor joists should be 2 × 6s, 2 × 8s, or 2 × 10s, depending upon the spans used. Center girders will be necessary for a house of any size; construction is as for any house at this point. Sheath over the joists with exterior plywood—¾ inch, or ⅝-inch for finish flooring on top. Be sure to use double joist headers all around so there is an adequate nailing surface for the first log course.

Permits and Cost

You will need a building permit from local authorities for your log house, just as you would for any residence, so get this in order before you start. Take a sample blueprint from one of the manufacturers to the authorities to secure a building permit. Also check out electrical, plumbing, and heating work thoroughly and get the required permits for this work.

40. *Interior of a kit log house.* (COURTESY ALTA INDUSTRIES)

41. *A handsome fireplace is part of this kit-type home* (COURTESY ALTA INDUSTRIES)

Financing the log house should present little problem, and this is a big advantage that manufacturers' sales personnel emphasize. Getting financing for a log house you build yourself can be difficult, but with precut log houses from a reputable manufacturer there is rarely any question of getting a loan.

How much money do you save by having a precut house versus a conventionally carpentered house? Considerable. An average-size (about 1,000 square feet) log house runs about $12,000. Of course, to this base price the foundation and interior work (plumbing and electrical included) have to be added, which is at least another $5000 to $7000. So figure $17,000 to $22,000 total for your kit log house. A conventional house of 1,000 square feet costs a total of about $50,000 if you have it built.

The remainder of this chapter is typical installation and information data for a log house as furnished by Building Logs, Inc., of Gunnison, Colo.* It is being reprinted here to show you what to expect in the way of instructions provided by the log-kit manufacturers:

Installation of Foundation

Building Logs, Inc., supplies the foundation or basement plan for your Lok-Log home. It is very important that this plan be followed exactly, as a square and true foundation will speed construction of your home. The diagonal measurements should be equal in both directions, and the outside measurements should be exactly as shown on your foundation plan. The pier locations should be as shown on your plan, and 8 inches below the top of the foundation. If any of these measurements are not correct, ask your foundation contractor to correct them.

Sill Plate Installation

The floor-framing plan shows Building Logs' suggested method of installing your floor system. If it is followed, you should not run short of material for your system. Start with the 2 × 8 sill plate, which must be job-cut to length, and job-drilled to fit over the anchor bolts in your foundation. If your foundation is true, the sill plate should be laid with the outer edge flush with the exterior of your foundation. Should the foundation vary, adjust the sill to exact outside of your plan. If the foundation has dips or high spots, shim sill plate to level. Toenail all joints with two 16d nails. Tighten the nuts on the anchor bolts, and the sill plate is secured. If your home is to be set on a basement, Building Logs will supply a fiberglass sill

*By permission of Building Logs, Inc.

sealer to be placed between the basement wall and the sill plate.

Rim Joist Installation

Install the rim joist by toenailing directly to the sill plate each 24 inches and at each joint with 16d nails. Be sure to crown all lumber before installing. The outside of the rim joist should be flush and plumb with the sill plate. Measure in 2¾ inches from each corner for wall-bolt locations. All other bolts will be measured from these marks. Using the floor plan, showing the wall-bolt locations, lay out the remaining wall bolts and cut 6 × 1½-inch access pockets in the rim joist. These access pockets will be used in the future for tightening your wall bolts. If your home is being placed on a basement, or if you have adequate crawl space, the access pockets are unnecessary, as tightening can be accomplished from the basement or within the crawl space.

Girder Installation

Build the double 2 × 8 girder, following the detail shown on your construction plans. Be sure to crown all lumber. Girder joints should be directly over the piers, and there should not be two joints on any one pier (if triple girder is used, the outside boards may both be jointed over the same pier). Nail girder together with 16d nails, placing them each 24 inches at the top and bottom edges. Place pier sills on the piers and set and nail girder with 16d nails. It may be necessary to shim the girder to make it flush and level with the top of the sill plate. If necessary, use a shim at both ends of the pier and nail through the shim.

Floor Joist Installation

Using the floor-framing plan provided by Building Logs, mark off the floor joists and end blocking on the inside of the rim joists and the top of the girder. Be sure the layout is correct with the plans, or the plywood sheathing will not break on the center of the joists. End blocking should always be installed because it helps bear the weight of your Lok-Log walls. Crown each joist and set in place. Nail through the rim joist with two 16d nails, toenail into the sill plate with at least one 16d, and toenail the center into the girder using a 16d nail on each side of the floor joist. Place at least two 16d nails both top and bottom of each lap joint over your girder. Notch all joists and blocking that hit on bolt-access pockets and frame all floor openings as shown on your plan.

Bridging Installation

When required, bridging should be installed before the plywood sheathing. It is installed in the center of the span between the rim joist and the girder. Use two 8d nails on each end of each piece of bridging. The bottom end may be left unnailed, for nailing later, but the 16-inch center-to-center spacing on the floor joists must be maintained.

Subfloor Installation

Measure in 48 inches at both ends and snap a chalk line to start the first course of plywood by. Start laying plywood sheathing, following sheathing plan provided. Sheathing is laid out so that, normally, the piece cut off one end will start the next row. The plywood sheathing should always run perpendicular to the floor joists. Use 8d nails to attach the sheathing, with nails spaced approximately 8 inches apart on each joist.

Log Wall Erection

Measure in 2¾ inches (2¼ inches for 6-inch logs) from all corners. If all measurements of foundation, sill, and subfloor are exact, the X mark you make at this point will be on the centerline of the wall. Check the centerline marks with long tape on all sides, ends, and diagonally. Install precut and numbered bottom plates. Be sure you are reading your elevation plan from the inside or the outside as specified; verify by checking correct location of windows and doors. Set the corner plates, centering the end hole over centerline mark. Using a chalk line, mark the inside-plate line. Keep in mind that the plate should overhang the subfloor ¾ inch. Set the remaining plates and nail in place with 16d nails. Locate bolt and wiring holes and mark these holes on the subfloor and the edge of the plate. Drill these holes on through the subfloor, using at least a ½-inch bit.

Exterior Door Jamb Installation

When the bottom plates have been properly positioned so as to locate exactly the door location, cut out the subfloor and the floor joists as necessary to recess the door sill. Recess the door sill into the floor until the top of the sill will be flush with the top of the finish floor; this will provide a flat surface for your threshold. Install the door unit and brace it in a plumb position; then install logs to door T-jamb.

Lok-Log Wall Installation

Logs in the first row, on two opposite sides, fastened to the 2 × 7 bottom plate, are half-logs (S logs). Be sure you are reading your elevation plan from inside or outside as specified; verify by checking correct location of windows and doors. Lay out the first row of S logs according to your plan. Center holes in end logs over the holes in the plates. Toenail end and corner of log to plate, placing corner nail so locking notch (plug cut) will cover it.

Now you are ready to align and fasten logs that fill in between end logs; align holes in S logs with holes in plates. Toenail exposed end of corner S logs to plate. Adjoining log is held in place by toenailing at the joint and open end; caulk log ends at joints with a thin head of caulking. Recheck to be sure wall is straight.

Exact centerline is important on all walls. When one straight wall of S logs is completed, lay opposite or parallel S log wall or walls in the same way. Check the distance between walls, at both ends, to see that they are parallel and that the centerline of wall measurement is correct.

When all S logs are aligned and fastened, lay out bottom rows of full logs and align and fasten as for the S logs. Toenail. Toenailing at the corners is done on all rows of logs. Nail one row of logs to the row beneath, using 8d nails.

Lay up the numbered Lok-Logs, according to your erection plan, until you reach about window height; approximately six rows of logs. Caulk log ends at joints, and follow method shown for toenailing; remember that the Lok-Log wall must be free to settle down on the dowels and *do not* caulk or nail dowels into the holes. Use your level frequently, especially at the wall corners.

After laying up the first five or six rows of logs, check for plumb. It is best to plumb all walls at the corners. If all rows of logs do not touch a straightedge or level, tap ends of logs at the corner notch with a sledge (protect log ends from sledge marks with a board) until walls are plumb. If wall leans out, start at the bottom and work up.

Dowel Installation

The dowels in your Lok-Log walls are very important. They seal the joints where two logs butt together, provide alignment, and most important, will keep a log that has a spiral grain from twisting too much, and opening gaps in your wall. With walls plumb and about 4 feet high, you are ready to dowel at all points where logs abut or join in the walls, and *all* holes which will not have electrical wiring or bolts. So that you won't dowel holes to be used for bolts or wiring, check the marks you placed on the subfloor, and don't dowel at these points.

Taper dowel ends to prevent a sharp edge from catching on the edge of the log, which would keep the Lok-Log wall from tightening. Cut all dowels so the end joint will be in the middle of the log instead of even with the top, and cut all window dowels 2 inches short of the top of the log below windows. It is very important that dowels be countersunk under windows; the easiest way to do this is to measure from the bottom of the wall to the top of the log below the window with a dowel, and then saw it 2 inches shorter, taper the end, and insert it in the wall. Stagger dowel lengths, using 4-foot dowels in every other dowel hole, and sawing 2-foot dowels for the holes in between. This eliminates having a dowel joint at 4 feet around the entire perimeter of your house.

Assembling and Installing T-Jambs

Nail door or window header and sill to T-jambs, forming window or door frames (door units have been installed and plumbed) according to the opening numbers on your plan. One man can be doing this while others are aligning the first rows of logs and erecting them to window height. That way the assembled jambs will be ready when needed. Make sure T-jambs are not racked. They must be square (check diagonal measurements) and both legs plumb when placed in the wall. The easiest way to be sure they are not racked is to be sure all four corners lie flat on the subfloor when you assemble it.

Door T-jambs are placed in the dado at the openings after the first couple of rows of logs have been installed and plumbed. Window T-jambs are placed when two rows of logs above window sill are erected. After setting the T-jambs in place, plumb and brace them to ensure that they will not move. *Do not* nail T-jambs to logs; the logs must be free to settle along the T-jamb. *Do* nail the sill of the T-jamb to the log beneath it. Make sure it is properly aligned before nailing with 16d nails. All of the T-jambs in your log wall should be 1 inch to 2½ inches shorter than the actual log opening. This space between the header and the trim gauge is necessary to accommodate the settlement and shrinkage encountered in your Lok-Log wall.

The 1 × 7 trim gauge should be nailed into the log directly over the T-jamb or door unit before that log is permanently installed. Some of these logs will have a cutout the same size as the T-jamb, and the trim gauge will fit into this special cut. The remaining logs will have the trim gauge nailed directly to the points of the dap. Use 8d nails to hold in place. The purpose of the trim gauge is to keep the top trim from leaning back against the log wall.

Do not nail into the logs! Even in your finish work, trim should be nailed to the T-jamb only. The logs must be free to settle down around the openings, and even a light finish nail will impair the settling of the logs.

Completing Wall Erection

Continue to lay up logs according to your erection plan, laying up corners and solid sections of wall first, and leaving short sections between windows and doors until last. Be sure to keep the corners plumb. If they lean out the least bit it will cause "end gaps" between the logs going across the top of the door and window openings.

After making sure the first log over the top of each opening is properly aligned (plumb) with the logs beneath it, drive a 10-inch spike into each end of it to help maintain alignment. Lay up the remaining logs. The last log on the sides which started with a full log will be a P log (full log flattened on top), while the last log on the sides which started with a half-log will also be a half-log (dapped half). Use a 6-inch spike in both ends of all dapped half-logs to maintain alignment.

Install 2 × 7 top plate and nail in place with 16d nails (open-beam roofs will not have top plates). Finish doweling all dowel holes, cutting dowels off flush with the top of the top plate. Taper dowels, and be sure not to dowel any electrical or bolt holes. As your Lok-Log walls tighten, the logs will slide down over the dowels. Dowels do not have to be countersunk at the top, as the space between the top plate and the roof sheathing is adequate to prevent the dowel from hitting the roof when your logs tighten. If open-beam roof is being installed, dowels must be countersunk, as tie beams or rafters may sit on dowel holes.

Installing Wall Bolts

One-half-inch wall bolts are threaded on each end. Before inserting them in the log wall the threads on each end should be checked to ensure they have not been damaged and that a nut will screw on them. Screw the washer with the nut welded on it onto the upper end of the bolt (thread only until the bolt extends slightly through the nut), and insert the bolt through the log wall. Insert all the wall bolts in this manner (make sure you place the right-length bolt in the proper hole, as indicated on your floor plan), and then place the large washer and nut on the bottom of the bolt under the subfloor. Again, thread only until the bolt extends slightly through the nut (tightening will be done at the top this first time). Tighten the welded nut on the top as much as possible and then place two 16d nails in the drill holes provided in the washer. Nailing the washer to the top plate ensures that it will not turn in the future when you tighten your bolts. If, after tightening the bolts, there is an excess of bolt protruding, cut it off flush with the nut. If there is danger of rain before bolts are covered, either grease the top of the bolts, or cover them to prevent iron stains from running down the Lok-Log walls.

Future tightening of your wall bolts, as your Lok-Log walls settle or tighten, will be from the bolt-access pockets you cut into your rim joist, the crawl space under the floor, or the basement. Bolts must be tightened whenever the nuts become slightly loose, to ensure your Lok-Log walls remain tightly together. Use a standard ¾-inch box or open-end wrench to tighten bolts, and tighten them as tight as you can get them with this wrench (you will not twist them off). If the bolt runs out of threads at the bottom, the entire bolt will turn and thread itself up through the welded washer on the top plate. There is a total of 10 inches of threads on your wall bolts, so it is very unlikely that you will ever run out of threads.

Large windows or openings will have either a 15- or 18-inch bolt over them. This bolt goes through the logs, plate, and trim gauge over the opening, and has a welded washer on top and a standard washer and nut under the trim gauge. Tightening is accomplished in the settlement allowance.

42. *Kitchen of typical Alta log home.* (COURTESY ALTA INDUSTRIES)

Each manufacturer has its own set of detailed instructions on how to assemble the log house. Many have special patented features and devices typical only of their style of log house. There are many companies selling log houses, and it is impossible to say one is better than another. You will have to send for catalogs, read all information carefully, and make your own decision.

──────10──────
FIREPLACES, HEATING, UTILITIES, AND INSULATION

Whether you have a conventional house or a log house, you need heat and electricity, and there are various systems you can choose from. The heating system can be gas, solar, or electrical, and in the log home a fireplace is desirable. It is appropriate for the structure and half the fun of owning a cozy home. There is tremendous comfort in being in your log house in front of a fireplace when the weather roars cold outside.

Fireplaces

A fireplace is handsome and practical. Fireplaces are not usually very heat-efficient (most of the heat goes up the chimney with the smoke), but with today's fireplaces you can actually warm your home to some extent. Building your own fireplace is difficult and takes expertise; it is better to buy the fireplace unit—this gives you a great choice—and install it yourself.

A masonry fireplace or masonry chimney is an entity in itself; it must not be supported by any other part of the house—it must sit on its own foundation. Chimney heights above roof lines can vary, but they should be at least 2½ feet above an eaved roof and 4 feet above a flat roof.

[121]

43. This homemade brick chimney is beautifully done and blends well with the log house. (PHOTOGRAPH BY MATTHEW BARR)

The masonry chimney has a flue (an interior funnel) and outside masonry; the chimney should be 2 inches from any framing lumber and ¾ inch from flammable finish material. There should be insulation between framing and finish. Line the flue with fire clay, a type of mortar that resists heat and comes in many different shapes. Build flue linings before the rest of the chimney, and fill the space between the flue liner and brick with mortar. Seal joints in flue linings with mortar or fire clay. Some communities have certain codes that dictate how wide and high chimneys must be, so check first with local building authorities.

The chimney obviously goes through the roof; at this

juncture of roof and chimney, flashing must be installed. The top of the chimney should be sloped and finished with concrete so rainwater will flow off properly.

The depth of the fireplace should be about two-thirds the height of its opening, and the flue area should be at least one-tenth of the open area of the fireplace if the chimney is less than 15 feet high, one-eighth if the chimney is more than 15 feet high. For example, a fireplace 20 × 30 inches and about 34 inches high and 16 inches deep should have a flue about 10 inches in diameter if it is round.

The hearth is the front floor of the fireplace and is made of

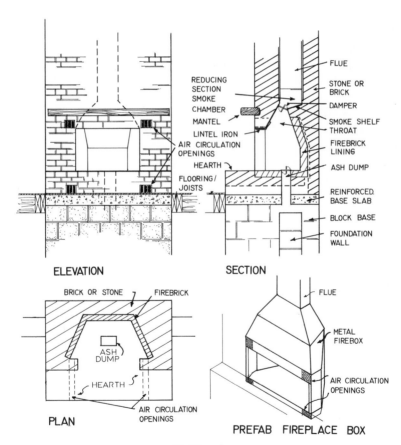

21. Fireplaces

tile or brick with its own concrete slab. The back hearth usually has an ash pit (dump) and steel door. The walls of the fireplace opening must be made of firebrick laid up with fire clay. Some fireplace chambers have angled sides, with the back wall straight for a portion of its height and then sloping toward the room for the rest of the distance.

A damper that can be closed when the fire is out to prevent warm air from escaping is located between the flue and the fireplace opening. Just behind the damper is the smoke shelf, which prevents smoke from looping back into the fireplace opening. The smoke chamber tapers up to the flue, and the top of the fireplace is usually supported by a steel angle iron (a lintel iron) set into the sides of the opening.

The fireplace must draw well so that smoke is carried by the warm air through the throat and out the flue. The smoke shelf keeps cold air out of the room by deflecting it upward. The cold downdraft is thrown upward by the damper. The damper can be bought as a complete unit in different sizes.

If you decide on a free-standing fireplace, you can choose an old-fashioned Franklin stove or one of the newer ceramic models. Some bolt into walls; others are floor-mounted, with suitable hoods over the opening and platforms under the stove. The Franklin stove, by the way, gives good heat and is not costly.

Fireplaces can be made in many different sizes and styles, and you can buy prefabricated units, which include a steel firebox.

Necessary Services

Along with the fireplace, which I think is essential to every log house, you must consider electricity, plumbing, heating, and insulation requirements. Because this is not a book on such subjects (there are many fine ones), here we give you just rudimentary knowledge, enough so you can talk intelligently with the electrician, plumber, or heating expert who installs the material (and I do recommend professionals for this work).

ELECTRICITY

The electrical aspects of your log house require more thinking than at first glance. For instance: What capacity amperage should a house have? For a home of 1,000 square feet, 125 amperes is usually sufficient, but this really depends upon how many appliances you have, your type of heating, whether or not you have air conditioning, and so forth.

Where the electricity comes into the house, install a meter, generally on the outside of the house. Service can be installed above or below ground, depending upon local codes. In the basement or a utility room have a distribution box with circuit breakers. The circuits have capacities from 15 to 50 amperes. Lighting takes a 15-amp circuit, heavy-duty appliances like dryers need 30 amps, and electric stoves require 50 amps. When the circuit shorts or trouble occurs, the circuit breaker trips and cuts off the electrical supply. Have enough circuits in your system to accommodate all electrical functions.

Because the number of switches and outlets will vary, as will the codes from state to state, again I recommend hiring a professional electrician.

HEATING

Even with a well-insulated wood house and a fireplace, some auxiliary heat will be needed unless you live in a temperate climate. What kind of heat? It depends upon a multitude of things. Probably the cost of fuel is the prime consideration these days. Electricity is expensive, and so is oil. Gas is cheaper, but again, the choice will depend upon where you live, how much heat you need in the home, and how large the house is.

In addition to fuel costs, you must consider *how* to heat: hot air, hot water, steam? Hot-water heat uses a central hot-water system that pipes by pump to baseboard radiators. Hot-air systems—much more popular—heat air through a furnace and by fans force the heat to ducts connected to room outlets.

In small log houses, wall-hung heaters can be used. They are inexpensive, easy to install, and do a fairly efficient job for their price. However, they are an eyesore.

PLUMBING

It is always economical to plan on placing plumbing lines and pipes as close to each other as possible. For instance, if there are two bathrooms, have them back up to each other or to a kitchen so they can share the plumbing pipes and the space where the pipes are hidden.

Plumbing involves getting water to the house, using the water, and then eliminating it. Plumbing pipes come in a variety of material, from plastic to galvanized iron. Copper is the best. There are certain techniques in installing lines and pipes, and because pipes are rigid, the work can be difficult and confusing. (Electrical wire is at least flexible.) The vent pipes and the toilet drains are the largest pipes. Plan plumbing so there is as little cutting of floor joists and such as possible. Joints should be cut only where necessary and then reinforced with plywood to ensure full joist strength.

All good plumbing requires vertical air chambers attached to water pipes in the walls at each fixture except the toilet. As with electrical work, it is best to let a professional take care of the plumbing in your log house. If you follow only the one rule of keeping the pipes in one area (with bathrooms back to back or a bathroom next to a kitchen), costs will not be exorbitant.

INSULATION

As mentioned in Chapter 1, the log house is relatively economical to heat because wood itself is an insulator; obviously a 5- or 6-inch log wall will protect against cold weather better than a frame wall will. However, even though the log house is insulated on its own, in most climates additional insulation will be needed. Insulation, which traps and holds air, is valuable in both cold and hot climates. Insulation keeps your home warmer in winter and cooler in summer, so you have less need for heating or cooling devices that cost money to use.

There are dozens of insulating materials available. Fiberglass is the most common and least expensive. Insulating boards work well but are costly. Blown-in insulating material, although convenient and fast to apply, is not applicable to most log houses.

By its very nature, the log house offers good insulation against weather; however, with today's heating costs, further insulation may be in order especially if you live in cold climates. Because energy usage is so important now, here are some notes to help you insulate your log house properly.

Insulation is rated by its resistance to heat and is called the "R-value." In short, the higher the R-value a material has, the better it will insulate. An 8-inch pine log has an R-value of 10.25. Today's insulating materials have the R-value marked on the packages. Look for them.

Generally, the National Bureau of Standards suggests R-11 insulation in exterior walls and floors and R-19 in ceilings. You might need higher R-values if living in either a colder or warmer region than average.

TYPES OF INSULATING MATERIALS

The basic types of insulating materials are, among others, fiberglass, rock wool, and polystyrene. (There are also loose-fill materials.) Fiberglass comes in blankets or batts and has an approximate R-value per inch of thickness of about 3.33; rock wall batts are slightly higher at about 3.66; and polystyrene boards measure 2.45 in R-value per inch of thickness.

44. On this level site a large log house presents a handsome picture; the hills in the background protect it from storms and overhangs are used as protection from intense sun. (COURTESY BUILDING LOGS, INC.)

The blankets or batts are fitted and secured in open framing in ceilings, floors, and walls; installation is simple. Boards are generally attached to ceiling or wall surfaces.

Blankets are best used for long runs between rafters or joists or in walls that are not of standard 8-foot thickness. Blanket thickness is either 3½ inches, having an R-value of 11, or 6 inches, with an R-value of 19.

The highest R-values are obtained in the first 3 inches of thickness; value declines as thickness increases.

Batts are simply blankets that have been cut into convenient size to handle precut lengths of 8 feet. They come in the same thicknesses as blankets and may be unfaced, faced on a single side with kraft paper or foil, or faced on both sides with foil and kraft paper.

The rigid board insulating panels are usually for exposed beam ceilings and are available in 4 × 8 foot, 4 × 4 foot, and 2 × 8 foot sheets. They are lightweight and have good insulating value for their thickness: ¾ inch to 4 inches.

Loose-fill insulation of various types is satisfactory, too, but generally difficult for the amateur builder to install.

Thicknesses required for R-values are:

Fiberglass	rock wall	
3½	3	R-11
6	5¼	R-19
9½	9	R-30 (two blankets or batts)

——11——

PRESERVE YOUR HOUSE

This may seem to be a superfluous section, but believe me, it is not. You should know a little something about insects and termites, because log houses (even with proper preventatives applied), whether of the kit type or home-made, need insect protection. Termites might like your house as much as you do!

Termites

Insects such as termites, post beetles, and carpenter ants are forever among us. Just where you live may make a difference as to how much trouble you will have, but eventually some insect that thinks your house is a meal will appear.

Subterranean termites cover a large expanse of land and appear everywhere except in the extreme Northeast, northern Michigan, and the North Plain states. The underground termite lives in wood and eats it and goes to the soil occasionally only to get moisture. Specifically, termites attack wood that is in contact with the ground, and if you have not built a proper foundation, they can attack your log house. And even if there is no wood in contact with the ground, some termites can build tunnels of mud to reach wood above the ground line. If you tap wood and it sounds hollow, termites are probably at work.

Dry-wood termites are not as common as the underground types, but they thrive in the Southern states. They are harder to control but leave sawdust as a clue to their presence. Termites are recognized by their thick waists and usually white or brown color. If you suspect either type of termite at work, call in reputable exterminators and let them determine what is going on.

Ants, Beetles, and Borers

Carpenter ants—not as common as termites—are a menace to any log house. They tunnel through wood but do not eat it. However, the small tunnels eventually become large ones and undermine the structure of a house. Because carpenter ants go back and forth, indoors and out, they are harder to get to or find than termites. Post beetles and borers are other wood culprits. All these insects should be eradicated when they are first noticed. These insects leave a trail of sawdust.

Fungi

What are fungi doing in a book like this? Plenty. Fungi, which are molds and mildews that grow in moist warm areas, attack wood and make it spongy, causing damage called dry rot. The rot is called "dry" because most damage is not caught until some time later, after the wood has dried. Decay usually occurs just below the surface of the wood and works its way into the heart of the wood. Thus, when selecting logs, "dry" is the key word. A fungus has a hard time attacking dry wood, but in moist wood it can have a ball.

Prevention

Prevention against insects and fungi is necessary. Good sanitation is one method of prevention. Do not let any holes around the foundation fill in with wood, and always remove any debris before backfilling the foundation—insects can get started in debris.

Wood should be at least 8 inches above the earth, and the bottom of joists should be at least 18 inches above the ground. I would add 6 inches to each dimension for real protection against insects. Be sure crawl spaces have vapor barriers or roll roofing on the earth floor. Lap polyethylene sheets 2 to 3 feet, and put the sheets up against the foundation walls at least 6 inches. Ventilate crawl spaces to discourage insects and rot.

Be sure foundations drain properly, to avoid excessive moisture and to prevent rainwater from running down house walls. Use gutters and downspouts to guide water away from the structure. Remember the two basic rules to avoid insects and fungi: no wood in contact with the earth, and no water trapped on horizontal surfaces at ground level.

GLOSSARY

Adze: Tool used to flatten portion of a log.

Anchor bolt: Metal spike projecting above concrete.

Ax: Tool used to notch and cut wood logs; several kinds.

Baseboard: Board or milled piece nailed onto wall at floor line. Also called mop board.

Batten: Narrow wood strip to cover joints in vertical boards.

Beam: Heavy horizontal timber or sill supporting floor joists.

Bearing wall: Any wall or partition that supports any load in addition to its own weight.

Blocking: Small piece of 2 × 4-inch lumber.

Board foot: Measurement of lumber—a piece of wood nominally 1 inch thick, 12 inches long, and 12 inches wide. A 1×12 a foot long contains 1 board foot. A 2×12 a foot long contains 2 board feet.

Bridging: Wood or metal members set between floor and ceiling joists midway in their span. "Cross-bridging" is a term for members installed in the form of an X; "solid bridging" is the term for nominal 2-inch members the same depth as the joists themselves and nailed at right angles to the joists.

Broadax: A type of ax used to flatten a portion of a log.

Building paper: Kraft paper used as insulation against moisture.

Caulking: Pliable material, dispensed from a caulking gun containing a cartridge, to seal beams, joints, and cracks, for weatherproofing and waterproofing.

Cleat: Metal hardware, usually U-shaped, applied to wood to support another piece of wood.

Collar beam: Nominal 1- or 2-inch boards connecting opposite roof rafters. Usually spaced every third or fourth rafter, and used to strengthen the rafter system. When collar beams are used for the ceiling under a roof, they are called ceiling joists.

Column: A perpendicular supporting member. Also called post or pillar; when made of concrete and a large size, often called a pier.

Concrete slab: Poured concrete used as floor.

Counterflashing: Flashing set into brick, usually chimneys, covering shingles and brickwork.

Countersink: To set head of screw or nail at or below surface.

Dado: A groove cut across a board.

Dimensional lumber: Standard board lumber such as 2 × 6, 2 × 8, for framing, etc.

Dormer: A roofed structure covering an opening in a sloping roof, with a vertical wall with one or more windows. Shed dormers have a sloping roof, with one dimension, and are designed to add more space under a roof. Gable dormers have a pitched roof and are designed primarily for light and ventilation.

Dovetail: Notch in wood shaped like a dovetail into which another piece of wood fits.

Drawknife: A tool used to strip bark from logs.

Flashing: Metal placed where roof meets wall or masonry, and in roof valleys, to weatherproof the joint.

Footing: Concrete platform, wider than the foundation, on which the foundation sits. Installed below the frost line to prevent heaving due to freezing and thawing. Can also support a concrete pier or other types of pillars.

Forms: Wooden members, made of plywood and 2 × 4s, used as retainers for concrete before it sets. Removed after concrete sets. Can be reused.

Foundation: Wall, usually of concrete or concrete blocks, that sits on the footing and supports the wooden members of the first floor.

Frost line: Depth to which ground freezes in winter. Ranges from nothing in the Deep South to 4 or 5 feet and more in extreme northern areas of the continent. Footings must be placed below the frost line to prevent heaving or movement due to freezing and thawing.

Gable: Roofline at the end of a double-sloped roof, forming a triangle from the peak of the roof to the bottom of each end of the rafters.

Girder: Heavy beam of wood or steel to support floor joists. Generally set into the sill and supported at intermediate points by columns.

Glazing compound: A modern putty used to waterproof panes of glass in a wood frame.

Grade: Surface of the ground.

Groove: A notch running the length of a board, on the edge.

Hatchet: A tool used to cut wood; gets into tight places.

Header: A beam placed at right angles to floor joists to form openings for chimney, stairways, fireplaces, etc. Also, a beam placed as a lintel over door and window openings.

Hip roof: A roof that slopes up from all four sides of a house, meeting at a point in the center or at a short ridge. There are no gables in a hip roof.

Insulation: Thermal insulation is placed in wall cavities, in attic floor spaces, and sometimes in cellar ceilings and between roof rafters to reduce escape of heat. It can be fiberglass (rigid or flexible), mineral wool, urethane or styrene, or any other kind of material that reduces heat loss. Sound insulation is of a similar material, mainly fiberglass, and is designed to reduce transmission of sound through walls, ceilings, and floors. Reflective insulation is usually aluminum foil in sheet form, designed to reflect heat back into a room, and to reflect outside heat in hot weather. It is ineffective unless an air space is provided between it and the interior wall. If it is used at all, it should be used with thermal insulation.

Jamb: Side and top frame of a window or door.

Joint: Any space between two components.

Joint compound: A plaster-type material, containing a glue, used to cover nailheads and joints in plasterboard wall construction. The joints are also covered with paper tape.

Joist: A floor or ceiling beam with a nominal thickness of 2 inches, and a depth of 8, 10, or 12 inches, used to support a floor or ceiling. Floor joists are set on the sill and on girders; if there is a second floor, they are set on top plates of walls. Ceiling joists are set on top plates, and there is no floor secured to them.

Joist hanger: Metal fastener used to secure the end of a joist directly against the side of a girder or other joist. Also called timber support.

Lap joint: A joint in which one member of a doubled beam or plate overlaps the other member. Most common in wall top plates, made up of 2 × 4s, with a lap joint at each corner.

Ledger: Strip of lumber nailed to a girder or joist onto which other joists are set. Also a heavy strip nailed to a wall as a joist support.

Log dog: A pointed metal rod that holds a log in place while you work on it.

Mortar: Material used to hold masonry together, made with Portland cement, sand, and lime.

Mortise: A slot or hole cut into wood to receive the tenon of another piece. The mortise is the female portion of a mortise-and-tenon joint.

Peeling spud: Does the same job as a drawknife, but is difficult to find.

Penny: Measurement of nails (originally English; indicated price per100). Abbreviated d.

Pier: Column of masonry.

Planed: Surfaced and smooth.

Plate, sole or floor: Bottom horizontal member of a stud wall, sitting on the subfloor. Top plate: top horizontal member, doubled, of a stud wall, supporting second-floor joists or roof rafters. Plates are used in vertical-log (stockade-type) log houses.

Polyethylene vapor barrier: Plastic sheets used to prevent moisture absorption.

Purlin: Horizontal member of a roof supporting rafters.

Rafter: A beam, nominally 2 inches thick, supporting the roof. A hip rafter forms a hip of a roof; a jack rafter is a short rafter connecting a hip rafter with the wall top plate, or a valley rafter with the ridgeboard; a valley rafter forms the valley of a roof, and usually is doubled.

Saddle notch: A saddle-shaped notch in a log.

Scribe: A measuring tool for marking wood.

Shake: A thick (split, now sawn) wood shingle, used for rustic siding and normal wood roofing.

Sheet-metal work: Nearly everything made of sheet metal, such as gutters and downspouts and warm-air ducts.

Shingles: Siding shingles are wood members sawn to a taper, made generally from red or white cedar and tapered from ¼ inch at the butt (bottom) to 1/32 inch at the top. Roofing shingles are made of asphalt, metal, slate, etc. Both types are manufactured to standard sizes.

Silicone sealant: Special compound sealant for joints.

Snowblock: A piece of wood set between rafters in roof construction.

Spline: A wood strip to fit in a slot or groove in a log.

Subfloor: Rough boards or plywood secured to floor joists, onto which a finish floor is secured.

Tie beam: Beam that acts as a tie in roof and holds the walls together.

Tie strap: Metal strip to join two boards.

Toenailing: Nailing at an angle, connecting one member with another piece perpendicular to it. Opposite of face nailing.

Tongue-and-groove: Lumber with tongue in one edge and groove in the other.

Truss: A set of rafters connecting opposite wall points.

Vapor barrier: Material, aluminum foil, kraft paper, or polyethylene, designed to prevent passage of water vapor through or into exterior walls. Always placed toward the heated part of the house. Insulation sometimes is made with a vapor barrier. If not, the barrier is secured after insulation is installed.

Weather strip: Any material placed at windows and door seams to prevent passage of air. Usually made of wood or aluminum with a vinyl seal.

MANUFACTURERS OF KIT LOG HOMES

Alpine Log Homes
Box 85
Victor, Mont. 59875

Alta Industries Ltd.
P.O. Box 88
Halcottsville, N.Y. 12438

Boyne Falls Log Homes
Boyne Falls, Mich. 49713

Building Logs, Inc.
P. O. Box 300
Gunnison, Colo. 81230

Green River Trading Company
Boston Corners Road
Millerton, N.Y. 12546

Hamill Manufacturing Company
Tacoma, Wash. 98421

National Log Company
P. O. Box 68
Thompson Falls, Mont. 59873

New England Log Homes, Inc.
P. O. Box 5056
Hampden, Conn. 06518

Northeastern Log Homes, Inc.
Groton, Vt. 05046

Real Log Homes, Inc.
Box 1520
Missoula, Mont. 59807

Vermont Log Buildings, Inc.
Hartland, Vt. 05048

Wilderness Log Homes
Rt. 3, HB3 D
Plymouth, Wisc. 53073

BIBLIOGRAPHY

The Wilderness Cabin, Calvin Rutstrum
    (Collier Books, N.Y., 1972)

Build Your Own Low Cost Log Home, Roger Hard
    (Garden Way Associates, Burlington, Vermont, 1977)

So You Want to Build a House, Peter Hotton
    (Little Brown, Boston, 1976)

From the Ground Up, John D. Cole and Charles Wing
    (Atlantic Monthly Press Books, Boston, 1976)

Walls, Floors and Ceilings, Jackson Hand
    (Harper and Row, New York, 1977)

How to Design and Build Your Own Home, Lupe Di Donno
    Phyllis Sperling
    (Alfred A. Knopf, New York, 1978)

In Harmony with Nature, Christian Bruyere and
    Robert Inwood
    (Drake Publishers, New York, 1975)

Hand Hewn House, William C. Leitch
    (Chronicle Books, San Francisco, 1976)

Other PLUME and MERIDIAN Books You'll Want to Read